The Theory and Practice of Academic Therapy

The Theory and Practice of Academic Therapy

The Role of Teachers in Promoting Mental Health

D. SAMUEL BUNN

RESOURCE *Publications* · Eugene, Oregon

THE THEORY AND PRACTICE OF ACADEMIC THERAPY
The Role of Teachers in Promoting Mental Health

Resource Publications
An Imprint of Wipf and Stock Publishers
199 W. 8th Ave., Suite 3
Eugene, OR 97401

www.wipfandstock.com

PAPERBACK ISBN: 978-1-6667-0162-3
HARDCOVER ISBN: 978-1-6667-0163-0
EBOOK ISBN: 978-1-6667-0164-7

08/12/21

For my mother Dorothy and my late father
Lt. Rusty Bunn (Fire Fighter), for every reason.

Contents

Contents

Preface: The Impact

TEACHERS HAVE AN OPPORTUNITY to make a significant impact on the lives of their students. Every semester for the past thirteen-years I have given my students an assignment called the "Gratitude Letter." To complete this assignment, students must choose someone who has been a positive force in their life to whom they want to express their gratitude. Within the letter students must cite specific reasons to justify their choices. This has been a fabulous assignment and I've received an abundance of feedback from students telling me how much they enjoyed doing this and how much they learned from it.

Each semester a significant number of my students choose a teacher as the person to whom they wish to express their eternal gratitude. This is impressive considering the competition teachers are up against to win this honor. This is compelling data which validates the value upon which students place their relationships with teachers.

Through all the years I've been giving this assignment, not a single student has ever indicated having chosen a teacher because of intellectual prowess. Without exception the reasons students give for writing gratitude letters to teachers include but are not limited to the following. The teacher's compassion, support, kindness, patience, encouragement, honesty, emotional availability, and empathy. Two additional comments I often see included in the letters are, "You helped me become the best version of myself," and, "Your believing in me, made me believe in myself." What higher compliments than these can a teacher receive?

Preface: The Impact

The student's have spoken. It's clear when they look back on what made their educational experiences meaningful, a strong emotional connection with at least one teacher is a major factor. Notably it isn't for their brilliance or effectiveness at executing their academic duties that teachers are acknowledged for. Conversely, it is an act of kindness, a supportive statement, or a demonstration of compassion that matters most. A touch of humanity in a potentially cold and indifferent environment. "What do patients recall when they look back on therapy? More often than not, they remember the positive supportive statements of their therapist."[1]

During the time that I've been giving this assignment, countless students have completed it. The outcome is always the same. In research terms, the results are reliable and valid. Being aware of the impact the relationship a student has with a teacher can have on the quality of a student's academic experience, motivates me to do everything I can to establish and maintain meaningful relationships with all my students. As a teacher, I work for the students, so their opinion of what makes for a meaningful educational experience is a driving force to my approach to teaching.

Having just read this information, if you are a teacher, I will now challenge you to take a moment and honestly reflect on the following question. If I were to gather all the students you have taught during your career and asked them to select someone to write a gratitude letter to, would any of them choose you?

Contained within this book, are the philosophy and techniques of my approach to teaching, called Academic Therapy. I have successfully used this method of teaching throughout my twenty-three years at the front of the room. I invite you to use them too.

1. Yalom, *The Gift of Therapy*, 13

Acknowledgments

FIRST AND FOREMOST, I want to thank God for blessing me with the gifts to teach, for putting the right people in my life to make that happen, and for the ability to write about it. I want to thank my mother for her constant support, and my father posthumously for the same. As always, I owe a debt of gratitude to Donna Zulch who has been a powerful and influential force in my life for the past thirty-one years and counting. I want to thank the administration at Marist College, where I teach, for renewing my contract from year to year. I would also like to thank the entire staff at Wipf & Stock Publishers for generously supporting my work. And finally, I want to thank the thousands of students whom it has been my privilege to teach and learn from over the past twenty-three years. It has been and continues to be my honor to serve you.

Introduction

I BEGAN TEACHING PSYCHOLOGY at the college level twenty-three years ago. At the same time, I was working as a psychotherapist. It didn't take long before I realized there was no significant difference between the students I taught in college, and the clients I treated via counseling. My students consistently disclosed to me via writing assignments, office hour meetings, and sometimes class discussions, they have many of the same problems as my therapy clients. In other words, they suffer. These problems included mental health issues like depression and anxiety. They also included addictions, trauma histories, eating disorders, abuse histories, learning disabilities, poor self-esteem, lack of confidence, broken families, poverty, physical illnesses, and more. Any teacher who thinks school is a student's only priority, or their top priority is naïve indeed. I dare say, with all the personal problems that many students are dealing with, it's miraculous they can focus on school at all.

Once aware of this information, I was immediately faced with a conundrum. As a teacher, it was not my role to get involved with my students on a traditional therapeutic level. I could not literally become a therapist for them. To try and do so would be unethical. On the other hand, was it any less unethical for me to be aware of human suffering and not attempt to do something about it? As a therapist I have a genuine concern for the human condition. I was compelled to take action. This motivated me to begin thinking of ways I could promote the mental health and emotional well-being of my students while at the same time teach them the required academic material. I concluded that although I couldn't provide traditional psychotherapy, I could create an academic experience for my students that would have a therapeutic effect. There was nothing unethical about that. And so, my treatment modality entitled Academic Therapy was born.

It is my intention in writing this book to put forward and illuminate a therapeutic approach to teaching. An approach that emphasizes the therapeutic value and healing nature that an emotional connection between teachers and students can have. Contained within this book are techniques that effectively facilitate meaningful relationships between teachers and students. Such relationships effectively promote the mental health and emotional well-being of students.

Many teachers may already be implementing these techniques, or ones that are similar. For them, this book will serve as validation and reinforcement that what they are doing is important. And for those teachers who are not doing so, this book will provide an opportunity to learn how to relate to students on a much deeper level.

CHAPTER ONE

The Student's Search for Meaning

STUDENTS SUFFER. THE EMOTIONAL pain that accompanies depression, anxiety, abuse, apathy, illness, etc. can be unbearable. Lack of meaning in the life of a student is typically either the cause of the suffering, or the result of it. This will depend on if the suffering is caused by internal factors like mental health/emotional issues or environmental factors like abusive relationships, broken homes, or poverty to name a few. From an existential perspective, finding/creating meaning in one's life, (a why), can greatly alleviate the discomfort caused by suffering and help a person cope with it more effectively via (a how).

Education is viewed as the main vehicle for solving the world's problems. It is endorsed as the ticket for creating a better future. Listen to any politician on the campaign trail and you will hear the promise, "I will make sure a quality education is available for all, so that everyone has an equal chance to succeed." But students don't gain inspiration from a textbook or a promise. They gain this from the meaningful relationships that are established with teachers, and the passionate example that teachers can demonstrate. A passionless teacher who just goes through the motions may effectively cover the academic material, but he/she will not motivate or inspire students to become better versions of themselves. They will not create hope or help alleviate the suffering of students. Students need education to be a meaningful experience that will put them in a position to create a life of success, happiness, and victory. It must be a reality. Teachers must motivate students to find their own personal why's that will help them cope with their various how's.

The late Dr. Viktor Frankl was an amazing person. During World War II, he and his family were separated and placed in various Nazi concentration camps. Upon his release from captivity, he learned he was the only member of his family who survived. He lost everyone and everything that was important to him. Despite this circumstance, he created a meaningful life for himself, dedicated to the service of others as an existential psychiatrist.

When explaining how he survived, he referred to the famous Nietzsche quote, "He who has a why to live can bear with almost any how." Frankl said that during his time in captivity, the belief that his family members were still alive, and he would one day be reunited with them gave him hope, or a "why" to live for. This in turn strengthened his spirit and will to live, thus providing the "how" he needed to survive the torturous conditions he was forced to endure. And while in captivity, he created meaning in the experience by devoting himself to assisting other prisoners. Another "why" which led to a "how." Clearly altruism can be an important factor in terms of creating meaning in one's life.

When a person like Viktor Frankl who survived such an ordeal says that creating a sense of meaning in the suffering, or a "why" to live for is the reason, it behooves us to listen. Nothing generates credibility more than experience. One of the key concepts Frankl gave us during his lifetime was called the "existential vacuum." According to Frankl, this phenomenon is the root cause of depression, despair, and emotional suffering. It refers to the feeling that one's life lacks meaning and has no purpose. In other words, for those unfortunate individuals, life lacks a "why."

Several questions can be raised here that apply to education and a student's academic experience. First, does this feeling of meaninglessness and despair impact students? Second, if so, in what way? And third, can we teachers do anything about it in the academic setting?

The answer to the first question is a definitive "yes." There is clearly a part of the student population that experiences a lack of meaning in terms of education and the impact it can have on their lives. Frankl observed, "Many a leading figure in education has become concerned with the boredom and apathy amongst students."[1] I have chosen to call this lack of meaning the "academic vacuum." Boredom and apathy in the academic setting, regardless of the catalyst, combine to contribute to the lack of meaning that many students experience.

Regarding the second question. The lack of meaning in the academic setting impacts students in several ways. One is behaviorally, and the other is emotionally. Students may react to the academic vacuum by displaying academic pathology in the form of maladaptive academic symptoms. These symptoms are manifested either behaviorally or emotionally depending on which symptom/s a student is engaging in.

And finally, regarding the third question which asks if we teachers can do anything to assist students who are displaying these symptoms and alleviate their suffering. The answer is, there is much that we can do if we are willing. The treatment for these symptoms is not found within a textbook. It is found within relationships. It is within the relationship between teachers and students that the techniques of academic therapy are implemented. All the techniques are based on clinical theory and relationship driven. The techniques and how to implement them are introduced and explained throughout the remainder of this book.

The first three questions lead to yet another. Can we as teachers address the symptoms generated by the academic vacuum by providing meaning for students directly? According to Frankl, the answer is no. He said, "Meaning cannot be given. What a teacher can give is not meaning, but rather an example of dedication to the cause of research, truth, and science."[2]

I agree with his assertion. Meaning cannot be given because of it's subjective and personal nature. It should not be imposed either, for to do so is to deprive a person of the opportunity and responsibility of creating their own meaning/purpose in life. Our task is to inspire and empower students. To motivate them via our example

---

1. Frankl, *Will to Meaning*, 86.
2. Frankl, *Will to Meaning*, 8.

to create their own meaning for their educational experience, and ultimately their lives. By demonstrating our passion for teaching, and perhaps other interests we have, i.e. music, sports, art, etc. we model what it looks like to live passionately, and the joy of having created that experience for ourselves. We show students what it's like to have a "why" to live for, that helps us as human beings to sustain our own personal "how's."

Students are the future. As the saying goes, "It takes a village to raise a child." Likewise, it takes passionate teachers to educate one. My challenge to every teacher is to take an honest look at yourself. What kind of teacher are you? What kind of experience do you create for your students? What kind of example do you set? Are you a passionate, supportive, and inspirational teacher whose company students enjoy? Do you take an interest in your students' lives? Do you model compassion, kindness, and patience? Do you teach lessons that assist students with passing the tests of life? Do the students see that you are truly invested in their success? Do you promote the mental health and emotional well-being of your students? All these things are necessary for academic therapy to work. The remainder of the book is dedicated to demonstrating how to incorporate these factors into your teaching.

CHAPTER TWO

Academic Therapy: A New Edition to the Therapeutic Family

AROMA THERAPY, PHYSICAL THERAPY, pet therapy, art therapy, music therapy, occupational therapy, speech therapy, play therapy, cognitive therapy. This is a short list of the various types of therapy that are available. Any activity or method of treatment that provides some form of relief from symptoms can have the word "therapy," attached to it. A review of the literature regarding various modes of therapy included all those listed here and more. But there was one therapeutic modality missing. A new edition to the therapeutic family I have chosen to call "Academic Therapy." I selected that title because it takes place in the classroom setting, and its purpose is to promote the mental health and emotional well-being of the students. Additionally, it can be readily implemented with students of any age group.

Until I thought to join them, the words academic and therapy were not connected anywhere. It seems they were a contradiction in terms. A computer search of the phrase academic therapy generated no results. Many books appeared which contained either the word academic or therapy within the title, but not both. Those respective works explained either the academic process involved in becoming a therapist, or various therapeutic modalities and how to use them. Not a single book suggested the relationship between teachers and students in the academic environment could be therapeutic. The publication of this book has eliminated that circumstance.

The Theory and Practice of Academic Therapy

What is academic therapy? I have defined it as, "any interaction between a teacher and student that promotes the mental health and emotional well-being of the student." I deliberately omitted making any reference to academic improvement because while this is often a secondary gain, it is not the purpose of this mode of treatment. The focus of academic therapy is on the psychological and emotional development of the students. In this realm, the areas of student development that are addressed include self-esteem, ego-strength, adaptive functioning, and self-confidence to name a few. To leave out that part of the academic experience that pertains to these areas of development in my clinical opinion is to be neglectful.

Many cultures place great value on education. So much so that one's level of academic achievement is used as a predicting factor for how successful a person will be in later life. A student who can conform to rules, complete assignments, pass exams, and perform well on standardized tests is perceived by educators as being healthy, well-adjusted, and prepared to cope with life beyond the academic setting. This way of thinking is not accurate.

Conversely, we tend to think if a student has a psychological or emotional problem, we will become aware of it via poor academic performance, behavioral problems, or both. This is also inaccurate.

During the twenty-three years that I've been teaching, I have learned one absolute truth. A student's ability to demonstrate a "normal" appearance, behave appropriately, and achieve good grades is not necessarily indicative of psychological or emotional well-being. Some students make their suffering known. Other students suffer in silence. The purpose of academic therapy is to create a supportive and therapeutic environment for students where teachers at best can alleviate this suffering, and at the very least, not make it worse. The techniques presented in this book can be readily utilized by teachers at the same time the required academic material is taught. It will enhance that process, not interfere with it.

CHAPTER THREE

The Academic Pathology of Everyday Students

ACADEMIC PATHOLOGY IS A term I use to describe the various academic symptoms that students experience that negatively impact their mental health and emotional well-being. A symptom is considered pathological based on the frequency of its occurrence and the destructive nature of its effect. When a clear and reasonably predictable pattern of behavior has been established, it's pathological. By giving a name and description to these symptoms, they become easily identified. Once identified, the process of providing interventions via the techniques of academic therapy can begin. I chose the word symptom to describe these issues as opposed to the word problem to avoid labelling the students. I subscribe to Carl Rogers' philosophy of unconditional positive regard. This means we accept the student without contingencies, while working with the student to alleviate the symptoms.

Academic symptoms are made up of two categories, behavioral and emotional. Behavioral symptoms are overt and visible. Emotional symptoms by themselves are covert and not visible. Emotional symptoms are often manifested and identified via engaging in a behavioral symptom, or something the students says. Sometimes there is a ripple effect, meaning resolving one kind of symptom may translate to providing secondary relief of another.

For the purpose of implementing academic therapy, it's not necessary to identify the cause of symptoms. As teachers, we are not permitted to proactively delve into the personal lives of our students. For example, we may never know if an overt behavioral symptom in school is being driven by a covert emotional symptom stemming from home. It is for this reason the techniques of academic therapy put forward in this book are universal, relationship driven, and apply to all students. Since we don't usually know which students are suffering, we will work under the premise that all students are suffering so nobody is missed.

The techniques put forward in this book are utilized in two distinct ways. One is publicly, via information that is shared with an entire class during lectures and activities. The other is privately during office hour meetings, e-mail exchanges, video conferences, and written feedback. It is typically during one on one exchanges and writing assignments that students disclose intimate details of their lives with a teacher. If we are going to find out the cause of a behavioral or emotional symptom, this is when it will happen. As stated earlier, that information is not necessary in terms of the techniques in this book being effective. However, if that information is obtained, it puts the teacher in a position to select specific therapeutic techniques that might be especially helpful to this person.

I have found the techniques of academic therapy to be highly effective in terms of assisting students who experience these symptoms to overcome them. For those who don't have any symptoms, these techniques are great for preventing them from happening in the first place. Students who are having difficulties will greatly appreciate this approach. Students who are fortunate enough to not experience difficulties will appreciate it also. In my experience, everyone likes to feel supported, understood, emotionally safe, and respected. Any teacher who chooses to implement the techniques of academic therapy into their approach to teaching are guaranteed to establish and maintain meaningful, therapeutic, and life changing relationships with their students.

CHAPTER FOUR

It's the Therapeutic Relationship That Heals: Here Is How to Build One

A THERAPEUTIC RELATIONSHIP BETWEEN the teacher and the students is the cornerstone of academic therapy, or any therapy for that matter. Without a strong connection there is no healing. I will also make the argument that in the absence of such a connection, effective learning does not take place either. Students will always invest themselves most in learning from a teacher they feel connected with, even if it's a topic/class they don't particularly like. For example, I once had a student who stated the following on an evaluation. "This class was a requirement for me. I was forced to take it and had no interest in it. I just wanted to get through it. But Professor Bunn was so passionate in his delivery of the material, and so invested in the success of us students, it ended up being my favorite class."

Supportive relationships don't happen by accident. With the appropriate knowledge base and genuine effort, however, anybody can build one. There are specific components that are necessary for this kind of relationship to happen. The most important point to keep in mind here is that one does not need to be a professional therapist to facilitate a therapeutic relationship. Academic therapy is not based on traditional sessions, lengthy intrusive explorations of the past, or insight into a problem. Academic therapy is based on the healing effect of a supportive relationship between teachers and students in a classroom setting.

The Theory and Practice of Academic Therapy

I will begin by listing the qualities a teacher must have to successfully generate a therapeutic relationship. Compassion, patience, empathy, kindness, and unconditional positive regard. These cannot be fabricated. Students are painfully aware of the difference between a teacher who cares about them, and one who doesn't. Tone of voice, choice of words, and affect/body language are where these qualities come out. A teacher must smile, remain calm, be mindful of his/her tone, be non-judgmental, and choose words carefully. Words are powerful. Words can hurt or heal. Words can build or destroy. Words can facilitate or isolate. Students are fragile, so please be careful with your words and behavior.

Next there is the issue of process and content. Content refers to the actual words that are exchanged between two parties. In this case, the academic material makes up most of the content. Process refers to the way the two parties who are sharing the material feel about each other. This can be observed via body language, tone of voice, and choice of words. Earlier I asserted that academic therapy can be provided without interfering with teaching the academic material, and this explains the reason. The tone of voice, choice of words, and affect/body language a teacher uses when interacting with students as academic material is being taught is where most of the academic therapy happens. When students have an appropriate yet strong emotional connection with a teacher, healing takes place.

Teachers have various tasks. One of them is to provide constructive criticism to students to help them improve. Being therapeutic doesn't mean avoiding problems. Supportive statements are an investment in the emotional bank account. Students will accept constructive criticism more objectively when they know the teacher truly cares and is offering said criticism with compassion and a genuine interest in helping the student improve.

CHAPTER FIVE

Therapeutic Factors of Academic Therapy

THERAPEUTIC FACTORS REFER TO those parts of the student we are attempting to strengthen via academic therapy. Students suffer from various problems in living. In our role as teachers, we are not typically in the position to help students solve said problems. In many cases we may not be made directly aware a problem exists, unless the student displays symptoms. Therefore, our goal is not to solve these problems, but rather to assist students to cope with them more effectively. The therapeutic factors that apply to our purpose here are the following. Adaptive skills, self-efficacy, and responsibility. By assisting students with strengthening these areas of functioning, we are empowering them to cope more effectively with any problems in living they may be experiencing.

We will begin by looking at adaptive skills. Adaptive skills are essential to good mental health and emotional well-being. They refer to the methods a person uses to cope with problems. As teachers we can assist students with developing adaptive skills. The adaptive (coping) skills a student learns to use with an academic problem in class can easily be translated to problems she may be having outside of class. By asking a student questions like, "How do you cope with receiving a grade you are not happy with?" Or, "How do you typically respond to criticism or conflict?" is an effective method for a teacher to explore and enhance a student's adaptive skills. Without intruding on a student's private life, the teacher can say, "That's a great coping skill. You could easily use this same approach to any issues you might have outside of school as they come along." Or, the teacher could say, "It seems like that way of coping is not working for you. Can we think of another technique you could try?"

Self-efficacy means, "I will succeed despite past failures and current obstacles." Teaching this concept to students early in the relationship and reminding them of it often is the most effective way to impart this. When I teach this, I always provide examples of well-known public figures who students know to be successful, i.e. Michael Jordan, then point out the various failures each suffered and overcame prior to becoming successful. I have found this empowers students and enhances their self-confidence. This gives them the ability to accept past failures without being destroyed by them and strengthens their "will" to overcome current obstacles and succeed.

Responsibility is another important therapeutic factor. "To be aware of responsibility is to be aware of creating one's own destiny, life predicament, feelings and, if such be the case, one's own suffering. For the patient who will not accept such responsibility, who persists in blaming others for his/her dysphoria, no real therapy is possible."[1] Students must learn to take responsibility for their thoughts, feelings, and actions. A student must understand the only person that one can control is oneself. When a student learns and accepts that he/she alone is ultimately responsible for success or failure in life, real learning has begun.

These core therapeutic factors are necessary to promote the mental health and emotional well-being of students. Improved self-esteem and confidence will be secondary gains here.

1. Yalom, *Existential Psychotherapy*, 218.

CHAPTER SIX

Clinical Pearls: The Foundation of Treatment

CLINICAL PEARLS. I LOVE that term. I wish I could take credit for thinking of it, but I can't. A former student used this term to describe the various motivational phrases that I imparted to her and her classmates. These are phrases that I share with each of my classes during our academic relationship. I require students to include them in their notes and commit them to memory. The purpose of my introducing these phrases to the students is to empower them. These phrases are powerful, easy to remember, and provide inspiration to the students. They are an essential part of academic therapy. They can be skillfully introduced by any teacher to their students regardless of the age of the student or the course being taught. They are universal principles. The sooner students learn and internalize them, the better off they will be. The following is a list of these clinical pearls and an explanation of what each means.

"I will not settle for less than I am capable of."

This phrase is intended to get students out of the habit of settling for mediocrity and stop letting themselves down. I want my students to get into the habit of making their best effort at everything they commit to as opposed to doing the bare minimum. Examples I give to the students of what settling for less than they are capable of looks like are the following. When your alarm goes off and you choose to go back to sleep instead of going to class, you have settled for less than you are capable of. When you have a test coming up and you choose to attend a party instead of studying, you have settled for less than you are capable of. I focus on how making these choices impacts them individually as opposed to others whom they might be trying to please (or not).

"I will not allow my desire for a better past to prevent me from creating a successful future."

In his book Staring at the Sun, Yalom refers to a patient who is so caught up in trying to change her past, that her emotional growth in the present is stunted. She can't move forward. He said, "Sooner or later she had to give up the hope for a better past."[2] Despite their youthful status, many of my students over the years have disclosed having very troubled pasts, full of abuse, mental illness, trauma, etc. The purpose of this phrase is to make my students aware that a turbulent past does not have to prevent the creation of a successful future, unless they allow it. I don't minimize their past/current difficulties in any way. But I want to assist them in getting out of "looking back" mode. I remind them regularly, through the use of this phrase, and Yalom's example, that a better past is not possible, and then I pose the question, "How much more of your energy are you going to spend trying to change history? Wouldn't it be more effective to instead learn from it and then create a better future?"

"I can't always choose what happens to me, but I can always choose my response."

I introduce this phrase to motivate my students to take responsibility for the one thing they can control, and that is their own behavior. People spend a lot of time trying to control others. I want my students to control themselves and get out of the habit of blaming others for their behavior/choices.

"Success lies in the effort, not in the outcome."

I introduce this phrase to my students because I want them to get into the habit of valuing effort more than winning and/or achieving. I say to them frequently, "If you've made your very best effort, then you have succeeded regardless of the outcome. In society today we place to much value on who gets the trophy, the promotion, or an A. I tell my students, if you have studied for every exam, written

2. Yalom, *Staring at the Sun*, 108.

every paper, attended every class, completed every assignment, and left out nothing you could have done to improve, then you have succeeded in this class. If having done all that you got a C, then your C is equivalent to an A, because you did everything you could. You made your best effort. I want them to take this lesson and apply it to all their endeavors. The lesson here is, do your best even if it doesn't guarantee a win, a specific grade, a promotion, etc.

"I can, I hope, and I wish are useless. Replace those phrases with I WILL."

I explain to my students that "can" only refers to potential. Theoretically anyone can do anything. "Hoping" and "wishing" will not generate an outcome. I have students write the expressions I can, I hope, and I will in their notes, and then put a line through them. Then I have them replace these with the phrase, "I will." Imposing one's will, implies that one will put something into motion. That one is going to take the necessary steps to make something happen, to achieve a goal, etc.

"I will embrace failure, and I will not fear making a mistake.

I introduce this phrase to my students to motivate them not to let their past failures to prevent them from continuing to try. I give them examples of great inventors and athletes who suffered many failures but continued to try and ultimately succeeded. Michael Jordan, James Harrison, and Alexander Graham Bell are a few of the people I use as examples of this. Students need to realize that failure is an inevitable part of life, but it doesn't have to prevent success. In fact, I encourage students to embrace failure, and not to fear making mistakes. I had a great supervisor who once told me, "You can only make a mistake if you are doing something. I would hire someone who takes the initiative to solve a problem and has the confidence to risk making a mistake doing so, over someone who stands safely on the sidelines waiting for someone else to solve it any time."

These phrases support the therapeutic factors of adaptive skills, self-efficacy and responsibility. When students internalize and apply these phrases in their lives, it promotes their mental health and emotional well-being effectively. The phrases should be introduced early on and repeated/reinforced regularly so they are not forgotten.

CHAPTER SEVEN

The Corrective Academic Experience

SCHOOL IS AN INSTITUTION where students go to learn new information and gain new experiences. The lenses through which new experiences are viewed are always at risk for being negatively influenced by the student's frame of reference. Frame of reference refers to the past experiences a student has had. These include positive and negative experiences. The experience itself does not create the problem. The outcome of the situation does. A student's frame of reference is powerful and has a direct impact on his/her level of expectation regarding how new experiences will end.

In traditional therapy, one of the goals is to liberate the client from the binding chains of the past. This process is facilitated via the therapeutic relationship and the creation of a corrective emotional experience. A corrective emotional experience is an event that challenges one's fears or expectations and leads to a healthy new outcome. While in treatment, a client will ultimately experience a problem/conflict in the present which mirrors one from the past. When the therapist guides the client through the issue to a healthy new outcome, a corrective emotional experience has taken place. Theoretically the client will then have improved functioning. Fear of the situation or ones like it will dissipate and no longer present a problem.

From a clinical standpoint, a classroom is to the teacher what an office is to a therapist. Students have problems that will surface and need to be addressed. Teachers have an opportunity to help students challenge their fears or expectations in the academic setting and lead them to new and healthy outcomes. A student may present an academic symptom in the here and now that reflects a conflict/problem from the past that wasn't resolved effectively. When the teacher guides the student to a healthy new outcome in the academic setting, I call this process a "corrective academic experience."

The academic symptoms a teacher encounters may vary in origin. It could be a problem left over from a previous academic experience with a different teacher. It could be a problem that originated from home and carried over into the academic setting, or it could be a combination of both. For example, the student who is pressured from home by her parents to get perfect grades. The problem stems from home but has implications in the academic setting. Since this is not a traditional therapeutic relationship, the teacher may never discover the true cause of the symptom. This lack of information will not prevent the teacher from being able to generate a corrective academic experience. Most corrective academic experiences take place without the teacher knowing about them.

Here is an example of a corrective academic experience I generated without knowing it. A student wrote to me and said the following. "Professor Bunn, other teacher's I've had criticized me and gave up on me. The way you kept telling me how smart I am, and not to settle for less than I am capable of, made me believe in myself again. Your support motivated me to not only do better in your class, but I did better in all of my other classes as well."

Until I received this e-mail, I had no idea this student lacked confidence. I did not know other teachers had been overly critical of him and essentially gave up on him. Students often suffer in silence and don't share their problems with us. This example reminds us that teachers can and do generate corrective academic experiences for students even when we don't know it. We must strive to support every student to ensure these corrections are made.

CHAPTER EIGHT

Therapeutic Opportunities: Addressing the Symptoms

THERE ARE TWO METHODS that I use to address academic symptoms with students. One is done publicly via classroom lectures and discussions. The other is done privately via office hour meetings, e-mail exchanges, and written communication that I provide through feedback I give on writing assignments. Every exchange between a teacher and a student is an opportunity to utilize the previously listed clinical pearls and therapeutic factors to promote their mental health and emotional well-being. To do this effectively a teacher must see and capitalize on such opportunities.

Public therapy is highly effective and using it one can reach all the students at the same time. Since we don't always know which students are having non-academic difficulties, this is a great way to reach everyone. I call this mode of treatment vicarious therapy. This may happen when I address the entire class, or when I have an exchange with a student in front of the entire class. Students always pay close attention to how a teacher treats other students. And any guidance, feedback, or support given to that one student has a positive impact on the others in terms of building trust with the teacher. I use these opportunities to demonstrate patience, compassion and empathy. I also throw in clinical pearls and therapeutic factors whenever possible. For example, I will say to a student in front of the group, "I want to acknowledge the outstanding job you did on that paper. You really went above and beyond. I respect that you didn't settle for less than you were capable of." Or, "That is an outstanding question. Thanks for bringing that up. Let's talk about that as a group." Or finally, "It's ok that you didn't know the answer to what I asked you. We are here to learn together. Let's see if anyone else in the group can help you out." When students witness positive supportive exchanges like those, it helps them feel comfortable, safe, and supported. They will be more apt to voluntarily participate and lose their fear of being wrong. I also threw in a clinical pearl there to reinforce going above and beyond is important.

Private exchanges also provide great opportunities to offer academic therapy in the form of support and the use of clinical pearls/therapeutic factors. Here is an example of an e-mail exchange I had with a student who demonstrated the cognitive distortion, "catastrophizing." She had two excellent grades in a row along with perfect attendance. When she received a failing grade on the next exam, she wrote me this e-mail. "Professor Bunn, I did much worse on that exam than I expected. Tell me what grades I need to get for the rest of the semester so I can at least earn a C." Her automatic response to one poor grade set a chain reaction into motion. Her thinking was, I got a bad grade, I'm not smart, I destroyed my chance for an A, I will now be lucky to get a C. Here is what I wrote back. I will call her Tina. "Tina, while it's unfortunate you didn't do as well on this exam as you had hoped, I want to remind you that your previous two grades were both an A. You are still in position to earn an A in this class. There is no evidence that will only earn a C. You WILL succeed despite past failures and current obstacles. One poor grade will not destroy you." She wrote back expressing her relief.

These are just a few examples of how to use public and private exchanges to demonstrate support and caring for students. In the context of these exchanges I corrected a cognitive distortion, implemented two clinical pearls, and alleviated Tina's fear. Successful therapy!

CHAPTER NINE

Take an Interest in Your Students' Lives

In June of 2017, a relationship that was very meaningful to me ended. The optometrist who had been taking care of my eyes for almost thirty-years announced his impending retirement. I will never forget how devastated I was when he said, "David, I need to tell you this will be our last appointment together. I am retiring at the end of the month." Naturally I was happy for him, but I was also selfishly feeling sorry for myself. He's been retired for several years now, and I still miss him. How is it that an optometrist whom I only saw for a total of thirty-hours in my life, had such an impact on me?

He was an exceptionally competent doctor whose medical judgment I trusted completely. Of course, that was important on a professional level. But on a personal level, which is where the power of a relationship is, it was because he took a genuine interest in my life. He examined my eyes as a matter of course, but truly cared about me. When I was with him, I never felt like I was just another patient on his schedule. While examining my eyes, he asked me about my job, my exercise routine, and my family. He knew I liked sports cars and motorcycles, so he would always ask, "What kind of car or bike are you driving now?" He in turn shared appropriate details about himself. He told me about his interest in photography, bicycling, and running. Or he would tell me about a vacation he had planned with his family. In short, we had a relationship that went beyond optometry, yet never violated any boundaries. He overtly demonstrated that he cared about me. His demeanor and personality had a tremendous impact on me. The way he treated me as a patient continues to influence me in terms of how I treat my clients and my students. He was more than just a doctor. He was a role model.

This is the same approach I take when interacting with my students. And to clarify here, there is no ethical violation of boundaries. Students are not required to share personal details about their lives with me. The supportive nature of the relationship I establish with them often motivates them to do so. And much like my former doctor, I share appropriate details of my life with my students too. This dynamic (process) adds an emotional quality and a touch of humanity to the relationship.

"Patients bask in the attention paid to the most minute details of their life."[1] To me, students and clients/patients are alike, and students do like it when I take an appropriate interest in their lives. I make a note of it whenever a student shares something with me and I will refer to it when appropriate. For example, a student once verbalized during class in September that her older sister was getting married in November and she was going to be the Maid of Honor. A task she was most excited about. On the Friday evening before she left town for the wedding, I sent her an e-mail that read, "Good evening. I just wanted to send you a brief note to tell you I hope you have a great time as Maid of Honor at your sister's wedding this weekend." That was it. She wrote back, "Hi Professor Bunn. I told you about that months ago. I can't believe you remembered the wedding is this weekend. That was very thoughtful of you. Thanks for thinking of me and I will let you know how it goes."

One more example. I had a student who was a pitcher on the college baseball team. He had shared the team was travelling for an important game. I had told the class that when I was growing up, I played baseball and was also a pitcher. I sent him an e-mail the evening before the team left that said, "Hello. I just wanted to wish you good luck in the big game this weekend. Throw strikes and trust your defense." He wrote back a similar e-mail thanking me for the thought.

---

1. Yalom, *Gift of Therapy*, 176.

These were just two examples of how taking an appropriate interest in the lives of my students helped to make the relationship more meaningful (process). Appropriate details of a student's life they will typically share include things like sports, music, hobbies, family events, etc. Sometime disclosures become more personal depending on the comfort level of the student. The point is to use whatever the student is willing to share as a mechanism to facilitate a deeper and more meaningful relationship.

Here are some comments I have gotten from students via evaluations of my class that relate directly to this issue. "Professor Bunn, taking the time to find out there is more to my life than just school is much appreciated." "Professor Bunn, I liked that you not only took an interest in us, but that you trusted us enough to share things with us about yourself." And a one more. "Professor Bunn, by establishing a relationship with us, you didn't just teach us about the power of a relationship by talking about it, you showed us by engaging us in one. Thank you." Take a genuine interest in the lives of your students. It's worth the effort.

CHAPTER TEN

Learn All of Your Student's Names, Quickly!

To establish a meaningful relationship with your students, you must learn their names. This is the most basic rule of effective communication. Regardless of your class size, you should be able to call each of your students by name by the end of week three, if not sooner. You must also use their names regularly to demonstrate this knowledge. Nothing makes a student feel less important than having a teacher who does not take the time to learn who he/she is.

Student rosters are typically available to teachers several weeks before classes begin. This allows time for a teacher to at least become familiar with the names of the students ahead of time. I began making a point of memorizing my students' names via the roster before the first day of class. This is half the battle, and it makes it easier for me to begin the process of attaching faces to the names when I meet them. It's alright to ask students for their assistance in this process. I say to my students at the beginning of the semester, "It's important that I get to know each of you by name. To help me with that process, when I call on you to answer a question or make a comment, please say your name before you answer. That will be very helpful to me." Students respond well to this request because it demonstrates that I want to get to know them. Additionally, it lays the groundwork for my philosophy of "collaboration equals success, "which is discussed in a separate chapter.

The reason I am making a point of discussing how important it is to learn your students' names is because students have told me via feedback that it's important. I have received a significant amount of anonymous written feedback from students on this issue, as well as direct comments contained within class reflection papers. In a reflection paper handed in by a student from a class I taught containing fifty-one people, the following comment was made. "Professor Bunn, I quickly realized that despite being an adjunct, you cared more about us than our full-time faculty did. You even took the time to learn all fifty-one of our names so you could speak to us directly. Not even most of the full-time faculty know our names like that, and they see us every day."

An anonymous piece of written feedback that was given to me early in my career demonstrates the impact of not learning the names of students in a timely manner. This student wrote to me, "I realized today that I must not participate in your class enough for you to know who I am. Today when I raised my hand and you called on me, you didn't say my name. I don't think you know it. I am going to start participating more so you remember me."

This was powerful feedback for two reasons. One, I should have known this students' name and I felt badly that I didn't. And two, this student blamed him/herself for something that was my fault, i.e. "I should participate more." The feedback should have read, "You need to do a better job of getting to know your students." This feedback motivated me to never make this mistake again, and I haven't.

I spent some time trying to figure out how to remedy this. Since the feedback was anonymous, (and I knew I did this with more than one student that day), I really could not identify directly who gave me the feedback. After much deliberation I decided to send out a group e-mail to the entire class which said the following. "I want to apologize for not having memorized everyone's name by this point in the semester. I have no excuse for this, and I am going to correct it. Today when I called on several of you, I was unable to do so by name. This is entirely my fault. It is my responsibility to know who you are regardless of how much you participate in class, and I am truly sorry if my not knowing some of your names was hurtful." That was the best that I could do, and hopefully it helped to remedy the situation.

Learn from my mistake. Understand that students need for you to know who they are. Being able to call on someone by name is a key factor in facilitating the academic alliance and establishing a meaningful relationship with your students. No student, even the ones who say or think they prefer it, should be able to make it through your class anonymously.

CHAPTER ELEVEN

It May Be Your Class, But They Are Someone Else's Children

A BRIEF BUT IMPORTANT point to remember here. As a teacher, parents loan you their children. They trust you to have their best interest in mind. They trust you with their child's emotional and physical well-being. I want you to be forever mindful of that. The most important responsibility a teacher has, is to keep the students safe. The age of the student has nothing to do with it. As a college instructor I teach young adults, and still their emotional and physical safety is my top priority during the time they spend with me. This kind of caring cannot be faked. Students are very perceptive, and they can readily tell the difference between a teacher who truly cares versus one who is just going through the motions. A student once wrote to me, "Professor Bunn. Thanks for genuinely caring about me. You are the first teacher who demonstrated you care as much about my success as I do."

So, before you raise your voice to a student. Before you carelessly say something abrasive that hurts a student's feelings. Before you embarrass a student. And before you treat a student in a rude, arrogant, or condescending way, I want you to remember this student is someone else's child. Be gentle. Be tactful. Be patient. You can offer constructive criticism without destroying someone's self-esteem. A parent somewhere has trusted you to educate this child while at the same time guarding this child's emotional well-being.

Do not violate this trust. To do so is a relationship felony. The parent may never find out you did so. And if the parent does find out, you may be lucky enough for this to be a parent who won't approach you about it, or worse yet doesn't care. But you can take my word for this. Student's do care, and student's do not give teachers a second chance in this arena. If you make this mistake, you can forget about ever gaining back the trust of that student. And if you are careless enough to behave this way towards a student publicly, every student who witnesses the exchange will cease to trust you as well. Please, acquire some emotional regulation and impulse control before you take a job at the front of the room.

CHAPTER TWELVE

Admit Your Mistakes: Doing So Builds Trust

I ONCE HAD AN appointment to have a crown put in by a dentist who appeared to have a great reputation. The walls of her waiting room were covered with numerous awards which were bestowed upon her for the exceptional job she did, and the quality of the service she provided. Certainly, the kind of things one wants to see before allowing someone to perform a dental procedure. Admittedly, going to the dentist causes me more anxiety than it should, so reading about how talented this person was before sitting in her dental chair was comforting. And when it was my turn to be seen, I bravely walked into her office and she proceeded to install the crown.

Eleven months later, while I was eating dinner, the crown suddenly and without warning popped off. Since it was located on the very last tooth in the back of my mouth, it was a miracle that I didn't swallow it, or even worse, choke on it. I gagged for a moment but ultimately coughed it up. I live alone, so had I choked there was nobody there to help me. It was a frightening and potentially life-threatening situation. I immediately made an appointment to have the crown replaced.

The next morning, I was in the examination chair when the dentist who installed the crown entered the room. I calmly explained to her in detail what had happened. I will never forget what she said. "Hmm. Well, I'm not surprised the crown fell out. But I am surprised that it didn't pop off sooner. You had a temporary crown that was supposed to be replaced ten months ago. The permanent crown has been here for months. We must have forgotten to call you. It won' take long to replace it but I don't have time today. See my receptionist on your way out and make an appointment. Good-bye."

I was stunned. No apology for the oversite. No empathy for my experience. She didn't even ask me if I was in pain as a result of the crown falling out. Furthermore, she DID NOT tell me when she installed the first crown that it was temporary. Had she done so I would have taken the initiative to follow up myself when I didn't receive a call from them in a timely manner. She glossed over the whole situation and went about her business like nothing had happened. She was so casual and arrogant I had to wonder if this was a common occurrence. What about all her awards for great service? Meaningless. A lesson in fiction. It goes without saying, I did not stop and see her receptionist. I walked out and never went back. Later that day a friend referred me to his dentist, and I had that person repair the crown. The new dentist did not accept my insurance plan, but I have stayed with him anyway and pay cash for my dental work. Amazingly, he is a great dentist despite not having a wall full of awards in his outer office saying so. Perhaps he is more secure in his ability and chooses to let his work speak for itself instead of relying on a plaque to do so.

"If you make a mistake, admit it. Any attempt to cover it up will ultimately backfire. At some level the patient will sense you are acting in bad faith and the therapy (relationship) will suffer."[1] And such was the case with this dentist. Had she apologized for the mistake and perhaps shown some empathy for what happened to me, I would have remained her patient. I know people aren't perfect. A routine phone call can easily be overlooked in a busy practice like hers. That I could forgive. But her arrogance. Her lack of concern. Her complete indifference to the entire situation. This I could not overlook. She lost me as a patient that day, permanently. As an aside, this was four years ago, and her office has not called me yet to inquire about replacing the crown.

---

1. Yalom, *Gift of Therapy*, 32.

In this example, I used an experience I had with a dentist to make my point. But the same refusal to admit mistakes happens in the academic world as well. As teachers, we are far from perfect. That's ok. Thankfully our students don't expect perfection from us. I've received a lot of constructive criticism from students during the past twenty-three years, and not once has a student said, "I'm disappointed you weren't perfect." However, our students do expect, and are entitled to a teacher's honesty and integrity. In the previous chapter, I explained how I didn't know the names of some students and the problems it caused. I could have chosen to arrogantly overlook that situation. I could have agreed with the student's perspective that if he/she had participated more in class, I would have known their names. I could have blamed the student for the problem. Instead I took responsibility for the error and publicly apologized to the entire class for it. It was the right thing to do. By acknowledging my error, I protected my integrity and I maintained the trust of the students.

Making an honest mistake in the classroom does not harm your credibility, compromise your integrity, or cause students to question your competence. But refusing to admit your error does all three. Students will forgive an error you that you humbly admit to and correct. They will not forgive your dishonesty or arrogance, nor should they.

CHAPTER THIRTEEN

Inquire About Their Past Academic Experiences

AS STUDENTS MOVE THROUGH grade school and college they remember most, if not all, of the teachers they've had along the way. Current teachers always pay for the sins committed against students by their former teachers. With that in mind, please conduct yourself in such a way that you don't make the job of future teachers more difficult.

Students will use their past experiences with other teachers as a frame of reference as they prepare for their time with you. I have found it is useful to inquire about the past learning experiences of my current students. "Once you become aware of the previous therapist's (teacher's) errors, you can attempt to avoid repeating them."[1]

This approach has been very useful to me in my classroom. By inquiring early in our relationship what the students found helpful or not, in terms of their past learning experiences, I can build upon what was effective for this group of students. I can also skillfully avoid repeating tactics that were not helpful to them.

When I solicit for anonymous written feedback from my students regarding this issue, I say, "I am curious about your previous learning experiences. Please tell me what teaching strategies you have found to be most beneficial to you, as well as things that didn't work for you. To keep this safe, please don't share names, just

1. Yalom, *Gift of Therapy*, 21.

experiences. Having this information will help us to create together the best possible learning environment for you. Thank you for your assistance with this."

It's as simple as that. By doing this, I establish trust, and I demonstrate that I care about the quality of the learning experience my students will have with me. I also get great some great new teaching ideas from each group of students. I have noticed over the years many similarities in terms of what students cite to be helpful in terms of presentation styles they prefer, teacher personality traits they like, and how they want to be treated. The more teachers are willing to learn about the wants and needs of students, the better they become at meeting those needs and providing an optimum learning experience. And some final benefits to this technique are it demonstrates concern for the student's well-being, builds trust, and facilitates the academic alliance.

CHAPTER FOURTEEN

Set Initial Goals and Objectives: Refer to Them When Problems Arise

ON THE FIRST DAY of class, I ask my students to write down personal goals and objectives for the class. This is a commitment to themselves in terms of what they expect to achieve and what they will do to achieve it. The students write this on the first page of their notebooks so it's the first thing they see each time the open it.

Periodically I will ask my students at the beginning of class to take out and review this information. This is especially useful to do after the first exam is handed back. I have found students don't truly take the semester seriously until the first major grade is earned. This grade will either validate the student's effort or be a wake-up call that changes are necessary. This is the time when students begin making appointments with me to discuss their concerns.

"The reasons for seeking therapy given in the first session may serve you in good stead during difficult phases of therapy."[1] Reviewing the initial goals and objective the student asserted on the first day of class, is very beneficial during difficult phases of learning, i.e. earning a poor grade. Such a review is usually enough to remind the student of what he/she initially chose to commit to, and why he/she needs to keep that commitment to succeed. I advise using this technique. Nobody's words influence a student more than his/her own.

---

1. Yalom, *Gift of Therapy*, 184.

To me students and clients are alike. I consider the initial goals and objectives that a student puts forth on the first day of class to be the equivalent of the initial complaint that a client puts forward in traditional therapy. I have found it's useful and necessary to revisit these with students when academic symptoms arise and begin causing problems (the difficult phase of therapy). I know from experience that despite my request that students review their initial goals and objectives regularly, they seldom do it.

Here is an example of an office hour conversation I had with a student who made an appointment with me directly upon receiving a mid-term grade she was upset about. I will call her Tracy. When she came to see me, she said the following. "I don't understand this Professor Bunn. I must be doing something wrong. I feel like I am doing everything in the class just like you ask us to, but my grades have been horrible. I should have made an appointment to speak with you sooner. Now we are at half-way through the semester and I feel like I'm drowning."

"Ok Tracy. We can't change what's happened, but you seem to be on the right track now. This feeling of drowning you are having is going to help us solve this problem. I'm glad you are feeling that way." "Why? How can my feeling this way be good." "Do you remember what we talked about in class regarding distress?" "Oh, oh that's right. You said distress was good because it means a person is desperate and open to change." "Excellent. That's right. I think we can substitute the word drowning for desperate here. Would you agree?" "Yes. Definitely." "Good. Your level of discomfort tells me you're ready to make a change." It was at this point referring to her initial goals and objectives came into play.

"Tracy, a few moments ago you said you feel like you are doing everything in class that I have asked. Is that correct?" "Yes, I really have." "So, you have evaluated what you are doing. Now let's look at perhaps what you are NOT doing." "What do you mean?" "Please take out your notebook and turn to page one. Tell me what you see there." "I see the long-term goals and objectives you asked us to write on the first day of school." "Outstanding. Would you please read them out loud?"

When I asked Tracy to read her goals and objectives out loud, she was hesitant. She sat in silence and reviewed them to herself for a moment, then she did as I asked. When she was done sharing, I asked her the following, "Have you kept your commitment to yourself Tracy?" "Have you done all of those tasks consistently as you promised yourself you would on the first day of class?" "No Professor Bunn. I guess I haven't." "Well Tracy, I think the answer to why you feel like you are drowning in my class, at least in part, is right there in front of you. I think the solution to this is right there in your own words. You came up with a fabulous plan on the first day of class. Now you just need to commit to following it."

Tracy was not exaggerating here. She was in fact drowning academically in my class at that time. However, as a result of that meeting, and her finding the motivation to follow her own advice, not mine, she got herself together and made significant improvement. And while she did not earn an A, I think she learned something much more important. She learned the importance of keeping one's commitments. This is but one example of how referring to the initial goals and objectives helps to resolve problems during the difficult phases of the academic process.

CHAPTER FIFTEEN

Use Reinforcement to Encourage Successful Behavior

WHILE IN SCHOOL RECEIVING our own academic training, teachers are exposed to theorists who studied the process of learning. These theorists are Watson, Skinner, Pavlov, and Bandura. There are others, but these gentlemen are typically the primary focus. In studying their respective theories, one of the factors we learn about is reinforcement. There are three driving principles about behavior a teacher must be familiar with. One, behavior that is not reinforced will not be repeated. Two, the best predictor of future behavior is past behavior. And three, all behavior is purposeful. That is, all behavior is goal oriented. There is always a payoff. The appropriate use of reinforcement requires planning, and for the teacher to know each new group of students well.

Since a primary goal of mine in the classroom is for the students to become motivated to succeed, I use reinforcement constantly. Reinforcement when used properly, is supposed to increase or maintain the frequency of a desired behavior. Reinforcement is a fast, convenient, and highly effective tool. I have found the use of intermittent reinforcement to be a powerful tool in terms of helping to create a meaningful relationship with my students. Using it wisely facilitates trust, increases self-confidence, and motivates students to always do their best.

As a refresher, I will briefly explain how positive and negative reinforcement works. Positive reinforcement is when something is added following a desired behavior, for the purpose of increasing or maintaining the frequency of that behavior. Negative reinforcement is when something is taken away following a desired behavior, to increase or maintain the frequency of that behavior. With reinforcement, positive and negative don't refer to good and bad. They refer to adding something or removing something respectively, to increase or maintain the frequency of a desired behavior. The following are some examples of how I use reinforcement effectively with my students.

I periodically send out e-mails to my entire group of students during the semester to show my appreciation for their hard work, and to boost their confidence. Here is an example of one such e-mail that I sent out on a Friday afternoon. "Good afternoon everyone. I want to commend all of you for such a great week. You all worked exceptionally hard during our last two class sessions which made for a fabulous learning experience which I thoroughly enjoyed. I am proud of you, and I hope you all have a great weekend." This was an example of positive reinforcement. Most of the students in the class wrote e-mails back to me, thanking me for acknowledging their efforts.

Here is an example of positive reinforcement that I provided to an entire class in person. "I just finished reading your latest writing assignment. I wanted to tell you as a group that your papers are spectacular. I was incredibly impressed by what I read. It is clear you all took this assignment very seriously, and I am looking forward to facilitating a group discussion about how it felt to write those papers during our next class session. Thank you."

I also provide positive reinforcement on an individual basis, both via e-mail and in class. In class I always publicly acknowledge my appreciation when a student makes a comment or answers a question, even if what was said is not on the mark. For example, "Sarah, that was an excellent guess. Your answer isn't quite what I was looking for, but I can see why you gave that response. You are thinking and that's important. Great try." This response makes the student who gave the wrong answer feel good about trying, and it sends a message to the rest of the class that it's ok to be wrong. I am looking for participation, not perfection. Another example, "Tom,

I really like your perspective on this. I have never thought about this concept that way before. That's excellent. Thanks for giving me something to think about."

And, an example of negative reinforcement that I have found useful. "Anyone who gets an A on the first three papers will not have to write the fourth paper." Another, "Anyone who has an A average at the end of the semester will be exempt from the final exam." In both these cases, I offered to take away something the students would gladly give up, if they performed at an optimum level throughout the entire class.

Sometimes because of how busy we become planning lessons, managing the classroom, etc. we forget the basics. We ask a lot of our students. We want them to behave, write papers, study for exams, hand in assignments on time, participate in class etc. but we don't always remember what we can do to facilitate that process more effectively. You may be saying to yourself, "Why do I have to reward my students for doing what they are supposed to be doing in the first place?" The answer, you don't have to do this. But if you do, you will find your students perform better, and your time at the front of the room will be much more rewarding for yourself, and more importantly, for them.

CHAPTER SIXTEEN

Do Your Own Research for Here and Now Classroom Application

RESEARCH PROVIDES VALUABLE DATA. If not for the people who enjoy engaging in the process of conducting research, humanity would still be struggling with many problems that have been effectively resolved via research. Despite how valuable research is, it does have potential drawbacks. Response bias, researcher bias, participant bias, and sample bias to name a few. The main issue I have with research in general concerns the generalizability of the results from a sample to the whole population. From a pragmatic standpoint, generalization is necessary, but not always effective.

It is for this reason that I regularly conduct my own research with each new group of students that I teach, and I propose that other teachers take the time to do the same. These are not major research studies, nor are they traditional. They do not entail a working hypothesis, nor a research committee to ensure the ethical guidelines of research are being followed. This kind of here and now research entails taking the time to solicit specific information from the group of students sitting in front of you. It involves finding out directly from the students what their needs are, what teaching strategies work best for them, what their concerns are, what they are hoping to get out of the course, etc. Naturally since people tend to have more in common than not, by doing this I learn teaching strategies that can be applied effectively to each new group of students that I get. However, that is not something that I take for granted.

The Theory and Practice of Academic Therapy

Each new group of students is unique. I want to know what their specific needs are so I can accommodate them as much as possible. By doing this I gain their trust, demonstrate concern for their emotional well-being, and create a comfortable learning environment.

The main method that I use to conduct this research is called anonymous feedback. "Since the feedback is anonymous, they (the students) are free to express anything they like without fear of retribution, and participation is completely voluntary."[1] This method eliminates response bias because there is no need for the student to feel obligated to say what he/she thinks I want to hear. And the issues of sample bias and generalizability are taken out of the equation as well.

This is a highly effective technique that I have been using for many years, which allows students the opportunity to make me aware of their wants, needs, concerns, expectations, disappointments, problems, etc. When I am given this information, I am in a great position to customize the class to ensure I've made the best effort possible to support my students and help them succeed. Students like being able to anonymously express their wants and needs. This process helps to facilitate the academic alliance and reinforces my "collaboration equals success" philosophy, discussed in a separate chapter. And finally, this directly addresses Erikson's third psychosocial stage called initiative vs. guilt. By not demanding, but simply asking for anonymous feedback, students have an opportunity to take the "initiative" to make their needs known and influence the direction the class goes. This is a great theoretically based lesson.

At the end of the semester, I discuss this point regarding Erikson directly. I say, "It is my hope that you each got exactly what you wanted from our time together in this class. If you took the time to express your needs via the anonymous feedback I asked for, this was most likely the case. However, if you chose not to take the "initiative" to participate in that process and therefore did not get something you wanted or needed out of the class, you alone are responsible for that. In that case I did not disappoint you, you

---

1. Bunn, *They Aren't Just Students*, 70.

40

disappointed yourself. Learn from that experience. When someone in a position to help you get your needs met, offers to help you do so by asking what your needs are, express yourself. If you don't the ensuing feeling of guilt and disappointment of having let yourself down is exactly what Erikson was referring to.

After each round of anonymous feedback received, I conduct a discussion with the students to process the information that was given to me. This demonstrates to the students I take their input seriously and took the time to read their comments. I tell the students which changes I will be able to make. I also tell them which changes I will not be able to make and explain why. This way, nobody who participates in the process feels unheard. The feedback I get from students at the end of the semester via reflection papers, and the comments they make on the evaluation forms given to them by the college include the following. "I appreciated that Professor Bunn asked us for feedback, and actually used our suggestions. It gave me a chance to participate in creating my experience." And, "By asking for our feedback during the semester, Professor Bunn was able to help us by making changes that benefitted us. Usually our evaluations aren't done until the last day of class, so suggestions we make might help the next group of students but do nothing for us. I think all teachers should do this."

CHAPTER SEVENTEEN

Collaboration Equals Success: It's Ok to Ask Students for Help

THE ABILITY TO WORK well with others. The confidence to offer a helpful suggestion. Being a team player. These are what it means to collaborate, and these are necessary skills in all aspects of life, i.e. work, marriage, parenting, sports, management. As teachers we tell students these skills are important. But telling students is not enough. For students to truly appreciate the power of collaboration, we must provide them with an opportunity to feel it. We must create situations in our classrooms where students must collaborate with one another, and we must also invite them to collaborate with us, the teachers. Students appreciate the impact of the lessons we teach when they are experienced in the here and now relationships we facilitate in the classroom. The following is an example of how I used my collaboration equals success with a group of students recently.

I was recruited to teach basic counseling skills to a group of fifty-one students who were studying to become Physician Assistants. The goal was to teach them how to apply counseling skills in medical situations while also demonstrating empathy and compassion. Doing role play activities was a necessary part of this process. With counseling, the academic understanding of the concepts and principles is necessary, but not enough. Nobody can learn how to effectively use counseling skills without practice. This group of students were gifted intellectually and highly motivated. They quickly memorized the terms and concepts which I presented to them. But as academically talented as they were, they needed a significant amount of practice to learn how to apply the techniques effectively. Role play exercise need to be supervised and critiqued. Therein was the problem. There were fifty-one students, and I was the only teacher. I had no assistance. I was at a loss in terms of how to effectively integrate and supervise role play activities with such a large group. How would I be able to observe each of them and offer constructive criticism? How would I evaluate progress? These were just a few of the problems I was faced with. And then I realized, I wasn't facing this problem alone. The students had to deal with this problem too.

I decided instead of dictating a solution to the students, the best course of action was to enlist their assistance. Afterall, these were highly intelligent people who were going to diagnose and treat complex medical problems for a living. They each had a vested interest in this class, and my thinking was surely this was a group capable of generating a solution to this dilemma. I had already introduced the concept of collaboration equals success to them earlier in the semester, as it applied to their future relationships with patients, families, and other medical providers. But this provided an opportunity for me to invite them to feel the power of collaboration in a here and now experience. This class met twice per week, on Tuesdays and Thursdays. So, one Thursday just before class ended, here is what I presented.

"Before we leave for the evening, I want to share with you a dilemma we have in this class. As you know, to truly learn how to apply the counseling skills we have been working on, role playing is necessary. Here is our problem. There are fifty-one of you, and only one of me. We need to figure out how to arrange our time together, so the role-playing exercises happen effectively. It is important to me that you each get the best learning experience possible. So, I am appealing to you for help. I want to collaborate with you to solve this problem together.

Please think about this between now and Tuesday. At the end of class on Tuesday, I am going to ask each of you to submit your suggestion/s on how to solve this, via anonymous feedback. I have expressed to you my philosophy of collaboration equals success, and this is a great opportunity for you each to experience it. I am looking forward to reviewing your suggestions and solving this problem effectively with you. Thank you."

The results were fabulous. I had fifty-one students, and I received fifty-one suggestions. Some students submitted several possible solutions. I took the feedback home and reviewed it for commonalities and pragmatism. I made a list of all the suggestion to present on an overhead projector at the next class so everyone would see their suggestion was considered. I then held a highly productive discussion with them in which together we came up with a multi-faceted approach to solving the problem. It worked out beautifully for everyone. Mission accomplished.

The clinical implications of this process are worth noting. By admitting there was a problem which I as the teacher did not know the answer to, I demonstrated humility and honesty. The students appreciated that. By telling them it was important to me they each get the best learning experience possible, I overtly demonstrated that I care about them. The students appreciated that. By collaborating with them to solve the problem by asking for and using their suggestions I provided two things. One, the opportunity to experience the power of collaboration. And two, the opportunity to take responsibility and play an active role in their educational experience. I ask my students for their assistance in solving classroom dilemmas regularly, and the results are always the same, fabulous.

From a theoretical perspective, I used Maslow's Hierarchy of Needs here. This process gave the students a sense of both esteem and belonging, which are both necessary components of achieving self-actualization. And I also incorporated Erikson's second and third psychosocial stages of development, which are autonomy vs. self-doubt, and initiative vs. guilt, respectively. The students had the autonomy to offer suggestions or not. They also had the opportunity to demonstrate initiative by offering suggestions to the problem. The students didn't know that Maslow and Erikson were at work here, but I did. And now you do. There should be a clinical/theoretical basis for everything a teacher does.

Here is some feedback that I have gotten from students over the years in which they chose to specifically mention my philosophy of collaboration equals success. "I loved helping to create this class. I really got to experience how collaboration works." Another comment, "Thank you for not trying to control us. It felt great to have a teacher trust us enough to work with us instead of against us." And one more, "I personally admired that you were willing to stand in front of the room and not only admit there was a problem you didn't have the answer to, but that you respected us enough to ask us to help find a solution. I wish more of my teachers could be that humble."

While it is not appropriate or pragmatic to always collaborate with students to solve classroom related problems, doing so whenever it's appropriate, facilitates the academic alliance, encourages students to take an active role in their educational experience, and certainly boosts their self-confidence.

CHAPTER EIGHTEEN

A Lesson About Integrity

IN MY CLASSES, I always discuss the importance of virtues and character. Both are necessary if one is to develop a positive self-image and a sense of self-respect. The virtues that I discuss with students throughout our time together include discipline, honesty, trust, patience, courage, discipline, and altruism. But I always introduce and discuss integrity first, because it is the most powerful of all virtues. It is the foundation upon which the other virtues are built. Without integrity, a person's word means nothing. I introduce this concept to my students on the first day of class. It fits in perfectly with my discussion about academic honesty, but I go on to discuss it on a much larger and personal scale. Here is how I initially introduce the concept verbatim.

I say, "Your integrity is the most important thing you have. It defines who you are. Your integrity is the only thing you truly own. You enter the world with it at birth, and nobody can ever take it away from you. Your car can be stolen, your identity can be stolen, and your wallet can be stolen, but your integrity nobody can take. People don't just lose their integrity by accident. People lose their integrity by choosing to give it away, piece by piece. Every time you lie, cheat, or steal, whether you get caught or not, you give away some of your integrity. Every time you settle for less than you are capable of, you give away some of your integrity. And every time you break your word, you give away some of your integrity. Integrity is not just for show. A person with integrity always does the right thing for the right reason, even when there is no tangible reward. Even when nobody will find out about it. A person with integrity makes personal sacrifices for the benefit of others and makes tough choices when easier ones are available. Integrity may not always bring physical comfort, but it always brings inner peace to the person who possesses it. And finally, integrity is what will motivate others to trust and respect you. If you choose to give away your integrity, you will never get it back. Therefore, my advice to you is from this day forward, choose to guard your integrity with all your strength. Never sacrifice your integrity for anyone or for any reason."

This is a brief but powerful lesson. Our students represent the future. What of value do we teach them if not about integrity? Two years ago, a student wrote the following random e-mail to me at the end of the semester regarding this lesson. "Professor Bunn, I just wanted to tell you the most important lesson I learned in your class was what you taught us about integrity. I had heard the word before and knew what it meant, but I never gave it much thought. After listening to what you said about it, I realized how important it is. It really is something that makes me trust and respect the people in my life who have it, like my dad, my coach, and you Professor Bunn. I wanted to thank you for that lesson. And to tell you that ever since you taught me that, I have decided to guard my integrity and never give it away, just like you said."

A teacher is a role model. I choose to introduce the concept of integrity to my students because I feel strongly about it, and I model it for them in how I conduct myself. Students watch everything we do and listen to everything we say, even when that doesn't appear to be the case. Tell your students about integrity. Tell them you expect them to conduct themselves with integrity. And always act with integrity yourself. If everyone would do this one thing, the world would be a much better place.

CHAPTER NINETEEN

Make Selective Observations About Their Work Performance

THE ABILITY TO GIVE constructive feedback to students regarding the caliber of their academic performance is crucial to their success and self-confidence. It is a skill within itself. For this kind of feedback to be effective, choice of words, tone of voice, and method of delivery is important. This is another area where the strength of the relationship between the teacher and the student (academic alliance) is critical. For when a student knows the teacher genuinely cares about his/her well-being, even a difficult message from the teacher will be well received.

I have found the most effective way to offer constructive feedback is to make what I call, "selective observations" about the students' work. It is not effective to limit the scope of a conversation to things a student needs to change or improve. Instead it is most effective to combine positive reinforcement to the student for what has been done well first, and then tactfully move into a discussion about what specifically needs improvement. This strategy prevents the student from feeling attacked and demonstrates to the student that I am on his/her side. I don't see the student from an all or nothing perspective.

"Avoid giving generalized feedback. Instead make it focused and explicit. Using parts is often a helpful device to decrease defensiveness."[1] I use this method effectively on a regular basis. The following is an example of an office hour conversation I had with a student that demonstrates the effective use of the "selective observation" technique. I will call the student Mike.

"Mike, you have many great qualities. You never miss a class, you are always on time, and you frequently make insightful comments during class discussions. That is all excellent. Having pointed that out, I want to express a concern I have about your written work. I've observed that your assignments are consistently handed in late, and sometimes they don't meet the minimum length or format requirements either. I've given this a lot of thought, and I'm having difficulty figuring out how you are so disciplined in one area of the class but seem to be slipping a bit in the other. I want to help you with this. Do you have any insight regarding this issue? Any thoughts or reactions to the observations I just shared with you?"

By explaining my concerns using selective observations, I prevented Mike from becoming defensive. I shared my positive observations first to acknowledge his strengths, then gently moved into pointing out the problem. This allowed Mike to hear my concerns about his writing assignments objectively. This approach showed that I respected him as a student, cared about him as a person, and had his best interest in mind. Three requirements for establishing and maintaining the academic alliance.

It turned out that Mike historically struggled in the area of writing. He had a great memory and effective reading/comprehension skills, but his writing needed work. His frustration about this caused him to procrastinate and avoid this kind of work. Procrastination and avoidance are two examples of "academic symptoms." His past teachers were satisfied to penalize him for the late submissions and the lack of quality of his writing assignments. They did not take the time to empathically address the problem the way I did. The supportive nature of this discussion motivated Mike to contact the college writing center and take responsibility for resolving this issue.

---

1. Yalom, *Gift of Therapy*, 119.

The Theory and Practice of Academic Therapy

Mike was painfully aware of his problem with writing. Before our discussion, he considered it a personal weakness and was ashamed of it. It was difficult for him to overtly admit he had a problem, but just a little objective support from me was enough to change his perspective and motivate him to seek help. And to be clear, I am in no way saying there is anything special about me here. My point is the technique is special. Any teacher who makes the effort can do this and generate similar results for the benefit of their students.

A year later just before Mike graduated from college, he wrote me the following. "Professor Bunn, I am about to graduate and before I do, I wanted to thank you for motivating me to get the help I needed with my writing skills. I struggled with writing all through high school, and in college as well until I met you. The conversation we had made me realize I should stop denying the problem and do something about it. Thank you."

Mike attached a copy of a letter he had written to a graduate program he applied to. It was comprehensive, expressive, and well written. I was very impressed. I don't know who ended up being happier about his improved writing skills, Mike or me.

CHAPTER TWENTY

The Spillover Effect: Confidence Travels

As a teacher, I have a responsibility to build up the confidence level of my students as much as possible. The very first motivational phrase (clinical pearl) that I share with my students is based upon Albert Bandura's concept of self-efficacy. "I will succeed despite past failures and current obstacles." I require them to write this in their notes and commit it to memory. I also repeat it as much as possible throughout the semester to make it stick.

I've discovered through the years that building the confidence level of the students in my class causes what I refer to as the "spillover effect." This takes place when the confidence level of the student in my class boosts their confidence in terms of their ability to be successful in other classes that perhaps they'd struggled in previously. It's gratifying as a teacher to watch students gain confidence and become increasingly sure of themselves. This improvement is indicative of the student gaining adaptive skills, the importance of which were mentioned earlier in the book.

An e-mail a student wrote to me on the subject validates this point. "Professor Bunn, I hate math and have always done poorly in it. I have a history of failure with that subject, so anytime I have a math test I expect to fail, and usually do. When you taught us, "I will succeed despite past failures and current obstacles," it not only helped me in your class, but in my math class as well. I did succeed in math this semester despite my past failures. I started approaching it with a confident attitude. I kept telling myself, I will succeed, I will succeed. I managed to get a C+ in the class. For me that is success, as I got an F in the last math class I took. Expecting to pass instead of expecting to fail helped with my test anxiety and I did much better."

CHAPTER TWENTY-ONE

Eliminate the "Hot Seat"

CLASS PARTICIPATION. EVERY TEACHER wants it. Most teachers require it. And some make it part of a students' final grade. Students logically expect that some amount of class participation will be required of them. So why is it so difficult to get it? Why does a teacher pose a question to a group of intelligent students, at least some of which know the answer, and get nothing but a sea of blank stares?

Numerous studies have shown that public speaking ranks very high on the list of things people are afraid of. This dread of public speaking is generated mostly by the fear of looking foolish in front of other people. In the case of students, it's the fear of looking foolish in front of their peers, and especially the teacher that is partially responsible for not speaking up. But there is another factor that must be examined here. And that factor sadly is the responsibility of teachers. Numerous students have reported to me via anonymous feedback they've had teachers in the past who have publicly yelled at them, embarrassed them, talked down to them, and generally made them feel badly when they have either given a wrong answer, or asked a question the teacher deemed foolish. I remember teachers doing that to me when I was in school. I guess not everything changes with time.

Erikson's first psychosocial stage of development is trust vs. mistrust. And safety is one of the steps on Maslow's Hierarchy of Needs. If we want students to participate in class via speaking up, we must proactively make them feel safe in doing so. In my effort to undo the damage done to my students by previous teachers when they have dared to speak up, I strive to create what I call a "corrective academic experience," (explained in another chapter), for them in my classroom. This entails putting the student in a position to engage in the behavior again, but to generate a healthy outcome and hopefully eliminate the fear, at least in my classroom.

To set up the corrective academic experience regarding the issue of class participation, I proactively begin talking about this on the first day of class. I want to create a safe and comfortable environment for my students and addressing the class participation component is crucial. Here is what I say verbatim to my students on the first day of class.

"In my class, I want all of you to feel safe speaking your mind, making comments, and asking/answering questions. If you don't participate on your own, I will eventually call on you specifically to answer a question. But you will never be on the "hot seat." There will never be any pressure. If you don't know the answer, or you would rather not answer, simply say, "I don't know," or, "I would rather not answer," and I will move on to someone else. It's not a problem. I will never embarrass you, criticize you, talk down to you, or make you feel foolish in front of your peers or me for any reason. I know you've probably had teachers in the past who have done that to you, but I won't. You have my word. We are all her to learn together. It's fine to decline to answer. It's also fine to give the wrong answer. It's ok to be wrong. In order to be wrong, you must be thinking, and thinking is the goal. From mistakes come wisdom. I welcome wrong answers because we learn from them together."

When I explain this, I can see a look of relief, and sometimes, disbelief come over the faces of my students. This speech takes away all the pressure, and sets the tone for a stress-free, non-judgmental learning experience. Naturally students don't really believe this at first.

I must prove this to my students by doing it. By the end of the first few class sessions, my behavior validates my word and class participation ultimately reaches an effective level.

At the end of the semester when I solicit for the final round of anonymous feedback from the students, I always get comments that relate directly to my "no hot seat" class participation policy. The following are some comments students have written to me verbatim. "I like that you didn't make us feel bad if we gave a wrong answer. It made me not be afraid to speak up." And, "It was nice that if you called on me and I said I didn't know the answer, that you said it was ok and moved on to someone else like you promised you would."

As teachers, we cannot reach our students intellectually until we make them feel safe emotionally. This kind of safety is easy to provide, and it generates fantastic results. It not only encourages participation, but it builds trust and strengthens the academic alliance. When your students trust that you will not do or say anything to hurt them, wonderful things happen. They will trust you, participate with you, and work hard for you.

As a teacher, I cannot do anything to alter the world my students experience at home, or at work, or even in other classrooms. But I do have the power to create the world my students experience with me in my classroom. Therefore, I ensure that world is safe and comfortable, just the way Abraham Maslow and Erik Erikson said it should be. What kind of world do you create for your students in your classroom?

CHAPTER TWENTY-TWO

Frame Your Responses Carefully

WHAT DOES IT MEAN to frame your responses carefully? Simply put, this means when a student answers a question, even when the response is incorrect, the effort is rewarded with positive reinforcement. Anytime a student speaks up in class, whether it be voluntarily or because of being called upon by me, I acknowledge the effort in a positive way. Consider the following examples of carefully framed responses that encourage participation and create a safe environment for the students.

"Steve, that's not quite the answer I was looking for, but I can see how you would make that connection. That's a good thought. While we are here, let's review that concept and then I'll get back to my other question." "John, that answer is not correct, but I find your conclusion intriguing. I am going to give your interpretation to that question some thought. Thanks for offering that response." And one more, "You are so very close to the correct answer Elizabeth. You're on the right track. Would you like to process this with me some more, or would you like me to see if any of your classmates can take this the rest of the way?"

Obviously positive reinforcement is important to give when students offer a correct answer as well. Here I emphasize finding creative ways to provide positive reinforcement when answers are not correct because the fear of being wrong is what I'm attempting to eliminate. I've never had a student yet who was fearful of being correct. The fear of being wrong can be very limiting, and it doesn't simply go away with age. As a teacher, one of my main priorities is to motivate my students to not only stop being afraid of being wrong, but to welcome it. My perspective on this is discussed in detail in a later chapter.

If a student offers a different perspective or interpretation of something we are discussing, I welcome that. Part of educating students is helping them to be confident and effective communicators. I want my students to understand that we can agree to disagree, and it will not have a negative impact on our relationship. Conversely, the mutual respect will strengthen our relationship. I say to me students periodically throughout the semester, "My thoughts about this may be different than yours, and that's ok. I don't require you to agree with the concept, I just require you to understand it. You can make up your own mind regarding what you accept or not."

To do this effectively requires some creativity and motivation on the part of the teacher. People who teach psychology, philosophy, sociology, and similar courses have more flexibility in terms of how something is interpreted or if an answer is correct, as opposed to someone who teaches math. Two plus two equals four, and when the student responds with anything but four as an answer, the answer is incorrect. There is no compromise. In cases like those the teacher can still offer positive reinforcement and encouragement as oppose to just saying, "that's the wrong answer." In this case the teacher has options like, "Terry, that's a great guess, but unfortunately that answer is wrong. Thanks for taking a shot at it." Or, Hmm, that was a good try Tanya. Before we talk about the correct answer, I'm curious to know how you determined the answer you gave. Maybe I didn't explain this concept as well as I thought I did."

Consider the top five obstacles to class participation that I've discovered during my years of teaching. Each of these interfere with answering questions, offering opinions, asking questions, or publicly disagreeing with the teacher. Each of these are eliminated by the techniques I have just discussed.

1. Being yelled at or embarrassed by the teacher for giving the wrong answer.
2. Fear of teacher retaliation for offering an opinion different than the teacher's opinion.

3. Fear of being judged as "foolish or stupid" by one's peers.
4. Being raised at home to believe questioning authority is disrespectful, so they don't.
5. Being a shy student who initially won't volunteer to speak. Calling on them helps.

The message here is encourage, support, and motivate. Encourage, support, and motivate. When you respond to a student who has just answered a question incorrectly, offered a different perspective than yours, or maybe even challenged your position about something, the rest of the students watch carefully to see how you handle it. When you respond with encouragement, patience, and emotional regulation, you create an environment where students feel safe to think independently, speak up freely, and participate enthusiastically. Eliminating the hot seat along with framing your responses carefully is the perfect combination for getting maximum student participation. I use these techniques every semester with great results.

CHAPTER TWENTY-THREE

Have Great Expectations: Raising the Bar for Maximum Results

THE LEVEL OF EXPECTATION that one has at the beginning of any endeavor is a powerful indicator of how the task will turn out. This is a concept from Albert Bandura known as reciprocal determinism. I have found this principle to be true in most areas of my life, including the classroom. I tell my students directly what my expectations of them are and why. Here is exactly what I say to my students verbatim during my introductory motivational speech on the first day of class, regarding this issue.

"My expectations of you are extremely high. This is because I respect you too much to set the bar low. It is better to aim high and potentially miss the target than to aim low and hit the bullseye. When you aim high, even if you miss, you will still do better than if you had hit a low bullseye. By my expecting a lot from you, you will get into the habit of expecting a lot from yourselves. You will become motivated to do your best all the time and get out of the habit of settling for less than you are capable of. You will no longer settle for mediocrity."

I always ask for anonymous feedback at the end of the first day of class to find out the student's questions, concerns, fears, expectations, and impressions of me. The initial feedback I've gotten over the years usually expresses two things. One, students are excited about the idea of making definitive self-improvement. And two, they are nervous or concerned that I will be difficult to please. This is excellent feedback and exactly what I am looking for. Both statements indicate the students listened to what I said and have taken it seriously. We are ready to begin our journey together.

By the time the semester is over, the anonymous feedback I get from students regarding the initial expectations I put forth on the first day of class typically change. Consider the following piece of anonymous feedback I recently received from a student at the end of a semester. "Professor Bunn, at the beginning of the semester I was convinced that by your setting the bar so high that I would let you down or disappoint you. Now I realize you expected so much from me not because you didn't want me to let you down, but because you didn't want me to let myself down. Thanks for motivating me to be my best self."

That piece of feedback sums up my purpose for overtly raising the bar perfectly. At first many of my students are nervous by my expressing how my expectations for them are so high. However, when the academic alliance between my students and I is established, students come to realize the purpose of getting into the habit of doing their best all the time is not about pleasing me. It is about pleasing themselves. I do get great satisfaction in watching my students use our time together to become better versions of themselves, but the reward of their efforts is strictly for them. A class is a journey of personal growth, no matter the subject. Developing the discipline to make one's best effort all the time and no longer settling for less than one is capable of is an integral part of that growth. Set the bar high, be supportive, and enjoy watching your students succeed.

CHAPTER TWENTY-FOUR

What They See Is What They Get: Do You Know What They See?

DID YOU EVER HEAR your voice on an answering machine and think to yourself, "Is that what I really sound like?" Or seen yourself in a picture or home video, and thought, "Is that what I really look like?" People don't typically know how they come across to others. For some professions, it is crucial to know how others see you. Teaching is one such profession. My question to you is, do you know how you come across to your students when you are teaching? Do you know how you really look and sound as you are directing your classroom?

I have been teaching at the college level for the past twenty-three years, as well as doing community workshops and trainings. I enjoy doing both very much. And I always thought I had an accurate picture of how I appeared to others while engaging in these activities until. . .

Seventeen years ago, I was invited to do a training called The Identification and Reporting of Child Abuse and Neglect for a large audience of mental health professionals who are mandated reporters of child abuse by law. I had done this training numerous times. It's one of my personal favorites because I feel very strongly about keeping children safe. When I arrived at the training site, the director of the agency which sponsored the training asked if I would allow the training to be video-taped, for the purpose of using the video as a training tool for future staff. I had no objections and did the training as planned.

The presentation went well. This group of professionals were very interactive. They were attentive and asked many great questions. As a group they had a lot of experience in the field, so I had the benefit of learning a lot from them via stories they shared, etc. The written evaluations I received were great, and I left that evening feeling that I had successfully accomplished my goal of effectively teaching this group of professionals how to identify and report suspected cases of child abuse.

Three weeks later, as an unexpected courtesy, the agency sent me a copy of the DVD they had made of the training. I was excited to watch it, as this was the first time a video had ever been made of me doing a presentation. I could not wait to see how it turned out. But then something troubling happened. . ..I watched it!

While the information I presented was exactly as it should have been, I was shocked at how I looked and sounded. This was not at all the way I pictured myself. Based on what I was watching, it was clear I had adjustments to make. A lot of them.

I noticed that when people asked me question, I subconsciously raised my eyebrows, and sometimes I would squint. At best this made me appear nervous, which I wasn't. At worst, these facial expressions may have appeared as me being judgmental towards the people asking the questions. Additionally, I noticed I said, "um" a lot. Ironically this is a pet peeve of mine when other people do this, so I was very surprise to find I was guilty of this myself. And finally, I noticed I spoke very quickly at times which may have made it difficult for the audience to keep up with me, especially if they were trying to take notes.

Once I got passed how traumatic this was for me to watch, I found there was tremendous value in this experience. Had I not watched this video I would not have been able to use it as a tool for self-improvement. Since I had already been teaching college for several years when this video was made, it was safe to conclude I had probably been doing these things on some level the entire time. I read my student and audience evaluations very carefully, and nobody had ever pointed out these things before. Regardless, I was aware of these issues now and something needed to be done.

I proactively went about eliminating these issues one by one. Despite my efforts, controlling my rate of speech when I present remains an issue. Now I tell my students and/or audience members at the beginning of a presentation that I am aware of this, and if they catch me going to fast, to please make me aware of it so I can slow down. I now spend time looking in the mirror at home to raise my awareness about my facial expressions when I am talking. I make a conscious effort to no longer squint or raise my eyebrows. I also began recording myself while lecturing to get a better understanding of my tone of voice and rate of speech.

Making these adjustments to my presentation style had benefitted me. I was already a confident public speaker but doing this helped me to be more aware of the way I come across to an audience and to feel better about it. Several years later I was taped again at a different event, and I was pleased to see my work had paid off. These issues that were accidentally brought to my attention had been all but eliminated.

It is my thinking that everyone who makes presentations, especially teachers, should periodically make videos of themselves while presenting for the purpose of evaluating how they look and sound to an audience. Nobody ever suggested this to me. I found out the value of this quite by accident. And this accident allowed me to learn some valuable lessons.

CHAPTER TWENTY-FIVE

Share Your In-Between Class Reflections

I FIND THAT I spend a significant amount of time thinking about my students and the events that take place in my classes long after class ends. Sometimes this happens when I'm driving in my car, taking a ride on my motorcycle, or when I'm out running. Occasionally a co-worker or friend will say something during a conversation that will remind me of something that was discussed in class. I think it's important to share these "in-between" class reflections with my students. It lets them know they matter to me, and that I take the time we spend together seriously. The following are a few examples of such reflections that I've shared with my students.

"Over the weekend I spent some time thinking about the conversation we had in class on Friday morning. I had a sense that class ended before we had a chance to finish the discussion. Does anyone have additional thoughts, comments, or questions about that topic before we move into new material today?"

Another reflection was, "During our last class, some great questions were posed to me. I really enjoyed that interaction. Upon thinking about this last night, I concluded I wasn't satisfied with one of the explanations I gave. I could have done better. I'd like to take a moment here to revisit that question and offer a more comprehensive answer."

It's not unusual for students to think teachers are just there for a paycheck, and to have summers and holidays off. Unfortunately, there are teachers like that and some of your students have probably been exposed to them. If you want your students to know they matter to you, and that you care about what you're doing, you must find ways to demonstrate that. I have found taking the time to share my in-between class reflections is a great mechanism by which to do this. If you want to truly understand the power of this technique, take a moment and remember how good you felt the last time you were talking to someone and that person started the conversation with, "I was thinking about something you said the other day and. . .."

CHAPTER TWENTY-SIX

Condition Students to Expect a Positive Experience

CLASSICAL CONDITIONING. A POWERFUL and empirically validated behavior theory. To provide a quick refresher here, classical conditioning put simply, is based on how people make paired associations. For example, television commercials often pair the image of football with drinking beer. This is done to motivate people to automatically associate watching football with drinking alcohol, and then proceed to buy beer in preparation for the big game. Food franchises do this too. McDonalds did not choose bright yellow as its trademark color randomly. The intent is to get people to think of McDonalds whenever they see yellow, causing them to hopefully go and buy a Big Mac or Happy Meal. These tactics work.

All of us are subject to conditioning. As teachers, we condition our students to associate certain things with us whether we try to do so or not. Therefore, it makes sense to use the power of association for the benefit of their learning experience. This is quite a simple lesson, but I've had great success with it. The beauty of this lies in its simplicity.

I provide my students with a highly predictable and positive experience. To do this I utilize three tactics. One, structure. Two, a positive attitude. And three, creatively making the material interesting. This takes work, personal initiative, and discipline, but the dividends are worth it. The following is an explanation of exactly how I do this.

Condition Students to Expect a Positive Experience

I begin every class the exact same way, without deviation. I stand in the front of the room and I say, "Good morning everyone," and then I pause and give a big and definitive smile which lasts for a few seconds to make an impact. This lets the students know I'm in a great mood, I'm happy to see them, and I'm happy to be there. Then I say, "Before we get into today's material, does anyone have questions or concerns about anything we've covered up to this point. Anything at all?" After doing that, I say, "Great. Now let's move into today's material." Then I proceed to lead the class in a discussion of the new material.

I end every class the exact same was as well. I always seem to run long, so I say, "Well, I see we are just about out of time. Thanks for your time and attention. You did a great job today. It's been a pleasure as always. Have a fabulous day."

I structure my class like a well written essay. It has a definitive beginning, middle, and ending. The predictability of the entire experience generates the conditioning. My students come to associate my class with a positive experience which will be interesting, personally beneficial, and stress free. This is exactly what I want, and I deliberately make this happen via my behavior and strict adherence to structure. The only thing that changes is the actual material that makes up the middle of the essay. But there is even consistency in that because while the material changes, I always make it interesting and thought provoking.

Students consistently tell me via anonymous feedback how much they appreciate how I teach. To be clear, they never say, "Professor Bunn, thanks for conditioning us," but the reference to the conditioning process is there. A student once said, "I like that you start every class with a big smile. It helps me relax and know everything is going to be ok, even on test days." Another wrote, "It's so cool that you begin every class by asking if we have questions or concerns about previous material before starting new material. I like that you make sure we all understand what we've done so far before just throwing new material at us."

This is how I condition my students to expect a predictable and positive experience with me. Teachers condition students positively or negatively. I always choose positive.

CHAPTER TWENTY-SEVEN

Give the Class a Title to Facilitate Meaning

To ME, A COURSE without a title is like a book without a title. It makes no sense. Had Peter Benchley simply called his book, "A Book About Sharks," very few people would have even picked it up. But "Jaws?" Now that's an interesting title that caught people's attention and aroused their curiosity. That's how I approach my classes. I give them special titles that spark student interest and arouse their curiosity.

All courses have titles assigned to them by a program, school, or department. Algebra, American History, Psychology 101. These are boring, generic titles that neither spark student interest or provide a greater meaning or purpose to the course. I teach psychology. The following are the special titles that I give my classes for the purposes mentioned above.

I call my Introduction to Psychology class, "Psychology in Action." This title fits the way I teach the material. In my class, I teach my students how to use the principles of psychology to create a life of success, happiness, and victory. I teach them how to put "Psychology in Action." I call my Child Development Class, "Creating the Future." Children are literally and figuratively the future of the world. I want my students who are studying to be teachers, counselors, etc. to remember that if you work with children, you are "Creating the Future." I called my Clinical Diagnostics class, "The Empathic Side of Medicine." I did this because while the students of this class were each going to become a Physician Assistant who works in the field of medicine, this class was not about medicine. It was about how to talk to patients. It was about how to establish meaningful relationships with patients, empathize with them, and demonstrate compassion. Therefore, by naming the class, "The Empathic Side of Medicine," the students were constantly reminded of what the goal of the class was.

To do this successfully a teacher needs only to be creative and think about what the greater purpose of the course one is teaching, is going to have for the student. For example, a math teacher might call a basic math class, "Numbers for Life," or "Calculating My Future," and remind students throughout the class how learning to do equations will benefit them personally in terms of balancing a check book, planning a budget, or saving for retirement. A gym teacher may call the class, "Creating My Body," and remind the students throughout the semester how all the activities they are doing benefit their physical health.

Giving the class a special title that better defines what the class is about helps a teacher create it, and helps student's see how the class will improve the quality of their lives. It gives them a sense of participating in something that was made especially for them. It gives them a different perspective on the class and provides a sense of meaning to it. As the late Dr. Wayne Dyer once said in a public presentation, "When you change the way you look at things, the things you look at change." An exciting and specialized title for a class changes the way students look at it. Much like an exciting title motivates people to open their minds to the contents of a book, an exciting title for a course motivates students to open their minds to the content of a class. My students consistently report liking these special titles and find them helpful in terms of making my classes more meaningful to them.

CHAPTER TWENTY-EIGHT

Be Tactful When Discussing Sensitive Topics

IN THIS CHAPTER I want to caution teachers who must cover sensitive topics to be careful when doing so. I can say with certainty that contained in every classroom is at least one student who is impacted by whatever sensitive topic you are covering. The list of such topics includes but is not limited to cultural issues, spiritual issues, sexual issues, addictions, mental illness, political views, etc. Being aware of this fact means that we as teachers must be respectful, objective, non-judgmental and professional in discussing such things. Our choice of words, tone of voice, and method of delivery are important to pay attention to, so that we can cover topics like these without hurting or offending the students in our classrooms who are impacted by them on a personal level.

I teach psychology, so when I am going to discuss sensitive issues like mental illness, suicide, ADHD, Autism Spectrum Disorder, etc. I am careful. The following is an example of how I introduce and discuss topics that can be emotionally charged and personal for my students. "Good morning everyone. Today we are going to discuss ADHD. This is a very prevalent problem, and it's quite possible that perhaps some of you are experiencing this yourself. Please be aware that in discussing this, no judgment is being passed. ADHD impacts each person who experiences it in a unique way, while also having some common threads. It's quite possible that when I describe the symptoms of ADHD and the impact it has on one's life, I may be describing you. Or perhaps you have ADHD and the information I share won't sound like you at all. I am mindful of your feelings and if you do have this issue and are comfortable doing so, feel free to share your experience so we understand it better."

I have found that beginning such conversations by overtly recognizing that students in the class might take the information and the way it is shared personally, helps people to remain objective. It only takes a moment to preface a lecture like this, and it demonstrates to the students that you care about their feelings. Students appreciate this.

Recently I gave a lecture on Borderline Personality Disorder, which is a very difficult problem to cope with. Often people approach BPD by focusing exclusively on the problems that people with BPD cause for others. When I discussed this, I used the approach I mentioned above. When talking about BPD, there is no way around explaining the problems it causes. However, I began the conversation by showing empathy for those who have it by pointing out how people with BPD suffer themselves, on a personal level. People often miss that point. I'm glad I didn't. Here is what a student said to me after class.

"Professor Bunn. My mom has BPD. Everything you just said applies to her, as well as my sister and I because we deal with it every day which isn't easy. But I wanted to thank you for how you talked about it. You described it perfectly without using words that make people like my mother sound like they are bad or broken. And you pointed out how they suffer too, instead of just talking about the problems they cause for other people. I just wanted to thank you for that."

Choice of words and being non-judgmental makes all the difference. When discussing addictions, I say things like, "A person who has difficulty with alcohol," as opposed to saying, "The alcoholic." One method of presentation is objective and empathic and the other judgmental and offensive. Taking the time to consider the feelings and life experience of your students when discussing such things will pay off. Think before you speak.

CHAPTER TWENTY-NINE

Pre-Semester Contact: An Invitation to Create the Class

THE ACADEMIC JOURNEY IS one that teachers and students take together. Proactively inviting students to help create the class sets the tone for a meaningful and collaborative relationship. It is a clinically based approach that meets several student needs by utilizing the theories of Maslow and Erikson. It also facilitates the academic alliance between the students and me. In doing so several clinical needs are met.

One, it gives students a sense of belonging and esteem, which according to Maslow are crucial if one is to reach self-actualization. Two, it addresses Erikson's first and third psychosocial stages of development, which are trust vs. mistrust and initiative vs. guilt respectively. Inviting students to share what their goals for the class are ahead of time shows that I care about their needs. Genuine caring facilitates trust. This invitation also gives students an opportunity to take the initiative to assert their needs thus creating an opportunity to get those needs met. All of this combined has implications for building trust, self-confidence, self-awareness, and personal responsibility.

In today's world, technology allows teachers to be able to use this technique quite easily. Students of all ages are on-line now and have e-mail addresses. All a teacher needs to do, is write an e-mail inviting students to share what they hope to get out of the class. The following is an example of an e-mail I sent to the students of a Child

Development class that I teach extending such an invitation. I sent this e-mail out three weeks before the class started.

"Good Morning Everyone. Welcome to Child Development. My name is David Bunn and I will be the instructor for the course. I am writing to each of you with a request. It is important to me that you each get the best learning experience possible, so I would like each of you to respond to this e-mail within the next week and answer the following two questions. One, what is your motivation for taking this course? And two, what do you hope to learn from taking this course? By sharing your responses with me, I will be in a better position to plan this course in such a way that you will each get the maximum benefit from taking it. Thank you in advance for taking the time to help me to plan our academic journey together."

My students typically have two reactions to this approach. One is shock. Students often report that none of the teachers from their academic pasts have invited them to participate in planning their learning experience. And two, gratitude. Students consistently report how much they appreciate my taking their individual goals into consideration when planning the course. When students help to plan the direction of the course, there is additional motivation for them to succeed. A secondary benefit to this approach is when students answer the question as to their motivation for taking the course, they will typically share personal information about their lives which helps me get to know them better. For example, a student once included in her response, "I have a brother who has an intellectual disability. One of my goals for this class is to learn how to better understand his problems and be able to help him as much as possible." Great. Sharing facilitates emotional intimacy and trust.

Based on student responses to the inquiry, I creatively present the course material in a way that applies to the specific needs and goals that have been expressed to me. This makes the experience students have in my class more meaningful. Teachers and students are on a journey together. It should be shared, not dictated. Collaborating to create what the journey will look like is beneficial to everyone.

CHAPTER THIRTY

The Power of Empathy: Never Underestimate It

EMPATHY HAS BEEN DESCRIBED in several ways. One is the ability to walk in someone else's shoes. Another is to be able to view something from the perspective of another person. Yalom asserts, "Therapy is enhanced if the therapist enters accurately into the patient's world."[1] Truer words have never been spoken. Empathy is the foundation upon which the ability to understand someone else is built. When someone feels truly understood, the relationship grows dramatically. Empathy is so important to a relationship, Carl Rogers cited it as one of his four therapeutic factors. I will assert here the relationship between teachers and students is enhanced when the teacher enters accurately into the student's world. A secondary benefit of this is, students are more motivated to learn from someone whom they feel truly understands them. I know this because my students have told me.

The ability to demonstrate empathy is not a prerequisite for becoming a teacher. I am not saying that a teacher must do this to be an effective educator. I am pointing out that if a teacher chooses to do this, students appreciate it. When a teacher demonstrates empathy, it strengthens the relationship between the teacher and student. As I assert throughout this book, the relationship between the teacher and student facilitates an optimum learning

1. Yalom, *Gift of Therapy*, 18.

environment. That is why I am proposing empathy as an integral part of that process.

Demonstrating empathy correctly is difficult. Even seasoned therapists sometimes struggle with this part of the therapeutic relationship. Why? Because the worlds our clients and/or students live in can be frightening. Their worlds often consist of addiction, abuse, mental illness, violence, physical illness, and poverty to name a few. To willingly enter that situation can be anxiety provoking and very uncomfortable. Therefore, to do so takes courage, curiosity, and some amount of emotional fortitude.

In my classroom, I use a two-prong approach to demonstrate empathy. One, I actively seek an invitation to visit the world of my students. I want to know as much about their lives outside the classroom as they are willing to share with me. I assign self-reflective papers which invite students to give me a glimpse into their worlds. A task they truly enjoy. And two, I overtly relate to my students in an empathic manner when I speak with them, both as a group and one on one. There are many opportunities to do this. For example, when I assign a paper, I say things like, "I am aware this is not your only class, or your only priority. You have other assignments to do, and you have other things in your personal lives to cope with, i.e. athletics, relationship issues, family life, jobs, etc. I appreciate your time, and I respect your willingness to always work so hard in here. Keep up the fabulous work."

The value of the papers is that I learn personal things about the students, and I get to demonstrate empathy via the written feedback I provide when I grade them. I always express my respect for how a student coped with a serious problem, etc. Additionally, if I've had a similar experience, I usually share that. Disclosure begets disclosure. I always conclude my comments on papers by saying, "Thank you for sharing this experience with me." As for the in-class comments, by consistently recognizing students have other responsibilities and priorities, students know I'm on their side. I feel for them, and I know being a student is a struggle. Never underestimate the power of empathy. It takes the relationship everywhere.

CHAPTER THIRTY-ONE

"How Does It Feel to Dish It Out?"
A Word About Displacement

THE COLLEGE THAT I have been teaching at for the past fourteen-years, Marist College, is also where I competed my undergraduate and graduate studies. A few of the faculty members from the Department of Social and Behavioral Sciences who are now my colleagues, taught some of the classes that I took when I was a student there. I must admit when I began teaching there it was a bit awkward for me. It wasn't the college itself or the student population that caused this awkward feeling. The catalyst was my suddenly becoming a colleague to people who were once in charge of me, so to speak. My anxiety was not warranted however, as the instructors I once had each welcomed me enthusiastically as I ran into them one by one.

During my first semester teaching there in the fall of 2007, I bumped into one of the instructors I just referred to. He was in my opinion the best teacher in the department and I was fortunate to have been able to take two psychology courses with him. He's had a powerful influence on my personal and professional life. He had become a full-time faculty member, but he was an adjunct who taught part-time and worked full-time as a therapist when I was his student. The exact situation that I have been in for the past twenty-three years. When I saw him in the hallway he said, "Hi David. I'd heard you were going to be teaching here. It's great to see you. Do you have a moment to come to my office and catch up a little?" I was

76

thrilled to see him, and even more excited that he was happy to see me. "Yes, that would be nice," I responded, and proceeded to walk with him to his office.

When I walked in and sat down, the first thing he said to me with a big smile on his face was, "So tell me, how does it feel to be on the other side of the desk, you know, and dish it out?" He was completely joking with this remark. He was always a fair, honest, and reasonable instructor. So, while what he said was a joke, it motivated me to start thinking about teachers who really do seem to enjoy "dishing it out," in an unkind way. Students spend a lot of time at the mercy of teachers in the academic world, and I think this is a point worth examining.

One of the many contributions that Freud made to the world of psychology was his notion of defense mechanisms. Here I will refer to the defense mechanism called displacement. Displacement takes place when someone is angry or frustrated at someone or some circumstance in their life, and takes that anger out on a different, safer, and perhaps powerless target. For example, a father gets yelled at by his boss at work. He cannot retaliate towards his boss, lest he risk losing his job. He in turn goes home and yells at his wife, or children. Or perhaps he will be nasty to the cashier who checks him out in line on his way home. Freud said that defense mechanisms were the mind's way of unconsciously protecting itself from shame, guilt, and/or anxiety. In the example just cited, the man would obviously be aware that he is being nasty to someone, but in theory he would not be aware of why. Or he would use another defense mechanism called rationalization to justify displacing his anger, i.e. the cashier was too slow, or was rude to him first. Perhaps he would accuse his children of making a mess, or his wife of "having an attitude."

Teachers are certainly at risk for engaging in displacement, and then rationalizing why it was done. If a teacher feels powerless in other areas of his/her life, is jealous of the students for some reason, or perhaps has their own unresolved issues, it is entirely possible the teacher will take out this frustration on students via displacement. As I reflect on my own career as a student, I can recall teachers who seemed perpetually angry, easily frustrated, and outright explosive. These teachers made a habit of yelling at students and making them feel badly. Additionally, when I was in school, I had witnessed unprovoked physical aggression towards students by teachers.

From a clinical perspective, this kind of emotionally, and perhaps, physically aggressive treatment from teachers has long-term repercussions. It prevents students from successfully achieving and moving through Erikson's first three psychosocial stages of development in the classroom setting. Those being trust vs. mistrust, autonomy vs. doubt, and initiative vs. guilt. A teacher who behaves this way, even occasionally, will prevent a student from trusting them, having the confidence to autonomously explore within the context of the class, or to feel safe taking the initiative to participate in the class via asking questions, making comments, etc. And regarding Maslow's Hierarchy of Needs, a teacher like this will prevent a student from feeling safe, or from developing a sense of esteem in that class. And worst of all, students tend to use previous learning experiences as a frame of reference for future ones. Therefore, a student who is treated this way by one teacher, may come to expect such treatment from others.

As teachers, obviously we spend time considering the academic success of our students. We must also consider how our behavior impacts the emotional and psychological development of our students. A teacher must act with emotional regulation and patience at all times, even when it's hard to do so. Some of the best lessons, we teachers pass on to students is how to conduct oneself with emotional regulation, and how to treat others with respect. Be mindful of your attitude. Be mindful of your tone of voice, choice of words, and method of delivery when conveying a message. And most of all, be sure to have all your "stuff" in check. If you don't, you will be at risk for displacing your frustration onto your students, and most likely use rationalization to blame them for it.

In closing this chapter, let's be sure that my esteemed colleagues' joke, "How does it feel to dish it out," remains just that, a joke. Instead, let's model patience, respect, empathy, and compassion for our students.

CHAPTER THIRTY-TWO

Extra Credit Assignments (No): Opportunities for Extra Points (Yes)

ONE OF THE LESSONS I have learned over the years is giving extra credit assignments tends to undermine the motivation of the students. Not the overachievers. With them I have found the opposite. They will do their best all semester long anyway, and then do the extra credit work just for good merit. But the students who have difficulty with making their best effort, extra credit seems to make the problem worse.

I used to provide extra credit assignments to give students who were not happy with their grades an opportunity to make an improvement before the semester ended. But I quickly learned that when students know there is a safety net to fall back on, their sense of urgency in terms of making their best effort throughout the semester diminishes. I also found it was difficult to generate extra credit assignments that were challenging enough to make the students work for it, but reasonable enough that it would provide the student with a fair opportunity to improve the final grade.

Eventually I decided to stop offering extra credit assignments. I clearly document my policy about extra credit assignments in my syllabus (treatment plan). Additionally, I explain my policy about this clearly on the first day of class and provide reminders about it throughout the semester. The reason for this, is that most students have been conditioned via experience to expect extra credit assignments to be made available to them. Therefore, I feel obligated to address this on the first day of class, and in doing so I also provide students with an explanation as to why I don't engage in this practice. Here is exactly what I say to every group of new students during my introductory lecture.

"In this class there will be no extra credit assignments, and I make no exceptions to this policy. Therefore, it is extremely important that you take full advantage of the opportunities that are given to you throughout the semester to score points. If you approach me at the end of the semester and ask if you can do an extra credit assignment, I will tactfully say no and remind you about this conversation." I always include that line because regardless of how strongly I state there will be no extra credit assignments, without fail, I always get at least one or two students every semester who make the request anyway. It's normal. Denial is at work here. "He said he wouldn't assign extra credit work, but I'm sure he didn't mean it."

After explaining that, I go on to let the students know that although I offer no extra credit assignments, I do offer opportunities throughout the semester for them to score extra points. For example, a week or so before a major exam I typically present students with what I call, "the extra points challenge." I will tell the students that anyone who scores over a ninety, will receive ten extra points, and anyone who scores over an eighty will receive five extra points. This gives students who are not capable of scoring over ninety a fair chance to earn extra points too. This has proven to be a great strategy that motivates students to study hard and do their best. Another opportunity I give students to earn extra points is to tell them on the first day of class that anyone with perfect attendance will get fifteen extra points. And occasionally when I give a writing assignment, I will tell the class that if everyone hands the paper in on time, then I will award the entire class ten extra points. They rarely pull that off.

I have found this "opportunity to earn extra points" much more effective than giving extra credit assignments for several reasons. One, it demonstrates to the students the power of positive reinforcement. I reward them with extra points following a desirable behavior to increase/maintain the frequency of that behavior.

Extra Credit Assignments (No): Opportunities for Extra Points (Yes)

Two, it keeps them focused on what they are responsible for within the context of the class in the first place. And three, it teaches them a valuable lesson about life beyond the classroom. If an employee makes his/her best effort all the time, a reward of a raise in pay or a promotion (extra points) may reasonably follow. But I have yet to hear an example where an employee who performs poorly is given an "extra credit task" so he/she can improve an evaluation before it's written or avoid termination. Life does not work that way. As a teacher, I am responsible for preparing my students for life beyond the classroom. Extra credit, in my opinion, is nothing more than a dangerous fantasy. I do not indulge that fantasy anymore.

CHAPTER THIRTY-THREE

Students and Teachers Are Equal Partners

Renowned therapist Carl Rogers was the first mental health professional to overtly make the assertion that clients and therapists are equal partners in the therapeutic relationship.

His thinking was that if a client was to learn how to establish and maintain meaningful relationships, then he and his clients needed to be on a level playing field. I agree with his perspective on this. This is the approach I take with my clients when I am providing therapy, and this is also the approach I take when teaching my students in the classroom.

It goes without saying that in a classroom, the teacher is the leader and has a responsibility to see to it the appropriate academic material is covered. The term I use to define the relationship I have with my students is "academic alliance." I make it very clear to my students on the first day of class that we are equals. I say, "You and I are allies. We are now involved in a relationship. We have different roles, but we are on the same team and working towards a common goal."[2] This approach is well received by my students, yet very unfamiliar because typically no teacher has ever overtly approached them this way.

The role of teacher is a powerful one. I have never felt the need to exploit that power by constantly reminding my students about it

2. Bunn, *They Aren't Just Students*, 30.

or behaving in a way that implies I think I am better than they are. Ironically, by my publicly relinquishing my power by inviting my students to be my equal partners on our academic journey, they respect me even more. I gain ground by giving it up. Saying we are equal partners is a great start, but it's not enough.

For students to truly believe we are equal partners, I hold myself to the same standards that I hold them to. And I don't just explain to them how this works. Talk is cheap. I put it in writing. My course syllabus of class policies and procedures explains in detail what my students can expect from me. The following are the policies I abide by to demonstrate to my students that we are completely and equally accountable to each other.

First is my attendance policy. If I am absent for any reason, each student gets an extra three points on the exam closest to the absence. Second is my policy regarding being on time. If I am late for any reason, each student gets an extra three points on the exam closest to my lateness. Third is my handing back assignments policy. I need one week to grade papers and exams. If I am not prepared to hand back those documents in one week, each student gets an extra five points on the exam closest to my being late handing back work. I am rarely absent, and I am rarely late arriving or handing back assignments. However, it does happen on occasion, and when it does, I impose the penalty on myself and the students get the points that were promised. I expect my students to attend every class, to be on time, and to hand in every assignment on time. If they fall short in any of these areas, there is a penalty. By penalizing myself for the same infractions, and in a way that benefits them, I avoid the act of being a hypocrite. Teachers must model the behaviors they expect their students to demonstrate.

A crucial factor that lends meaning to a student's educational experience is meaningful collaboration between the teacher and the student. We are equal partners on a collaborative journey.

CHAPTER THIRTY-FOUR

Catch Them When They Fall: Provide Support After a Failure

THROUGH THE YEARS I'VE found the most difficult task for me is to return an exam to a student which reflects a failing grade. I remember what it was like to be on the receiving end of those. It felt terrible. Knowing I am about to hand a piece of paper to a student that is most likely going to make him/her feel badly is tough. The reason is that I care deeply about the emotional well-being of my students. When they feel badly about something, so do I. If it's the first exam, I also worry about the impact a poor grade may have on a student's level of confidence and motivation to keep doing their best.

For example, I recently returned an exam to a student who earned a grade of fifty-seven. It was the first exam. He wrote an e-mail to me which said, "I can't believe I did this bad. Can I still pass the class, or do you think I should drop it and take it over next semester?" This came from a student whose attendance was perfect and who achieved an A on the first paper. He interpreted a fifty-seven as being much worse than it was. Not only was he disappointed with the grade, she went from striving for an A, to considering either failing or dropping the class. I see responses like these regularly. It is for that reason that I cultivated a strategy to help prevent situations like these from destroying a student's ambition.

This strategy is called, "Catch them when they fall." After I hand back the first exams, I always give the following pep-talk. "Now that I have handed back your first exams, I'm sure there are some of you who are not happy with your grade. This could be because you studied hard and expected to do better, or perhaps you didn't study enough or at all. Regardless of the reason, don't beat yourself up over it. I'm going to tell you all something, and I want you to remember it. This is only the first exam. No matter what you scored, each of you remain in a position at this point to earn a final grade you will be proud of. Don't let one performance you are not happy with destroy your confidence and motivation. Remember, you will succeed despite past failures and current obstacles. Use this as a learning experience to figure out what you need to change for next time to make an improvement. If you need assistance with that, let me know, and I will gladly meet with you to discuss it."

Academic therapy in action. I can see the overt relief in the faces of my students when I give this pep talk. I don't want my students to suffer and receiving a poor grade on the initial exam causes suffering. Hearing me re-assure them that everything can still be ok, and success is still within their reach, makes them feel so much better.

I want to mention here that I don't allow my students to be in denial about their academic standing in the class, nor do I sugar coat anything. If a student who has failed the first exam, goes on to fail the second and/or third one, an equally supportive conversation takes place, but in a difference context. In that circumstance I will have to objectively discuss with the student how the possibility of an A, or maybe even a B, is no longer within reach.

The purpose of the post-test pep talk is to prevent students who fail the first exam from wrongfully concluding success in the class is no longer possible. This assists students to maintain their motivation and typically try even harder. It also keeps their self-esteem in-tact. School is stressful enough. Part of keeping the anxiety level of my students down while increasing their self-confidence, is supporting them when they need it most. They need it most when they have just earned a failing grade. A student once wrote to me, "Thank you Professor Bunn for supporting me and not making me feel badly even when I failed."

CHAPTER THIRTY-FIVE

In Conclusion: The World I Create vs. The World They Go Home To

As a teacher, I cannot control the world my students go home to everyday. The only thing I can control is the world I create for them to learn in. I take that task very seriously. The world I create for my students is indeed a very special place. Physically it looks like any other classroom. Emotionally however the climate is much different than what most students experience in other classes, or so they tell me.

I create a therapeutic learning environment for my students. My classroom is a relaxed and stress-free place. We know clinically that anxiety interferes with a person's ability to focus on and retain information, so logically it makes sense to do everything in my power to eliminate those factors. I encourage my students to think critically and express themselves freely.

I treat my students like therapy clients. I talk with them, not at them. I validate their feelings, empathize with their problems, and offer them unconditional positive regard. I never talk down to them or embarrass them. I never do or say anything that would cause them physical or emotional harm. I always have their best interest in mind. I am completely invested in their success, and very protective of their emotional well-being. I've had students write to me and say, "I found your class to be therapeutic. I benefitted from this experience personally and I wish it wasn't over." I don't provide therapy for my students, but I provide a therapeutic environment which they feel and respond to.

In my classroom I utilize Carl Roger's client centered approach which involves his four therapeutic factors. Those being, empathy, active listening, genuineness, and unconditional positive regard. I am a professional therapist who teaches, but one does not need to be a professional therapist to utilize these most basic relationship techniques. I treat my students as equals, as Rogers did his clients. I relate to them in the most genuine way possible. My students never have to wonder what I am thinking, as I share my thoughts and feelings regarding the class and them openly. It is a real relationship. Naturally it is time limited, goal oriented, and contains all the ethical boundaries of the teacher/student relationship. However, this method of communication generates a true connection between the students and me which maximizes the potential for learning, healing, and reaching one's full potential.

In many ways I view my task as a teacher as being very similar to that of a coach. It is my intention and my responsibility to bring out the best in each of my students. I help them to look within themselves and see their inner strength and inherent value. I do everything I can to improve their self-esteem, increase their confidence, and ensure they believe in themselves as much as I do. The late and extremely inspirational Kobe Bryant once said, "What's important is to bring out the best in people so they can be successful in whatever they choose to do." Kobe Bryant was certainly a man who knew how to bring out the best in people, and I can't think of a better quote with which to end this treatise.

Bibliography

Bunn, David S. *They Aren't Just Students: Making the Connection.* Eugene, OR: Wipf & Stock, 2020.

Frankl, Viktor E. *The Will to Meaning.* New York: Penguin Books, 1969.

Yalom, Irvin D. *Existential Psychotherapy.* New York: Basic, 1980.

————. *The Gift of Therapy: An Open Letter to a New Generation of Therapists and Their Patients.* New York: Harper Collins, 2002

————. *Staring at the Sun: Overcoming the Terror of Death.* San Francisco: Josey-Bass, 2009.

www.ingramcontent.com/pod-product-compliance
Lightning Source LLC
Chambersburg PA
CBHW062344300326
41947CB00012B/1209